The Great Book of American Heroes

32 True Tales From American
History That Made Them Legends

Bill O'Neill

ISBN: 978-1-64845-065-5

DON'T FORGET YOUR FREE BOOKS

CONTENTS

INTRODUCTION

Welcome to *The Great Book of American Heroes*! In this book, you'll read about 32 of the United States' greatest heroes and heroines, who've shaped the direction of this country and helped make it what it is today. You'll learn about what made these exceptional people great and why they are considered heroes today, sometimes decades or even hundreds of years after they died. This book goes beyond the big events and brings you closer to the heroes themselves, revealing some little-known facts about these important people.

There are heroes and heroines from all walks of American life in this book: some who went from rags to riches and others who had plenty of privileges and opportunities and took full advantage to make themselves a success and leave their imprint on American history.

You've no doubt heard of or read about many of the people profiled in this book. This book examines some pretty important political personalities, including a few presidents, but does so in a way that will keep you interested. More than just a boring history book that recites fact after fact, this book brings you right into the heroes' lives and lets you experience all of their triumphs and failures on their way to influencing American society.

George Washington, Thomas Jefferson, and Martin Luther King Junior are just three of the American political heroes profiled in this book. And, since the United States has been known as a nation of innovation for more than 100 years, some heroes of American science are also explored. What would this country be without the likes of Thomas Edison, Benjamin Franklin, and Alexander Graham Bell? It would be a lot more backward, that's for sure!

As vast as America is geographically, it needed some pretty incredible people to explore it from coast to coast and beyond during the European settlement. You'll learn all about how Lewis and Clark explored what would become the West and how Charles Lindbergh and Amelia Earhart risked it all by flying into the great unknown.

Entertainment, sports, and literature are an important part of any culture, so we cover some of the true leaders of American pop culture. From important writers such as Upton Sinclair and Mark Twain to athletes and actors such as Jim Thorpe, Babe Ruth, and John Wayne, you'll learn how some of these people influenced their professions and changed the American cultural landscape in the process.

This book also covers important military leaders who fought for — and in two cases, against — the American government. The American experience has been complex and not every important American willingly went along with American expansion.

Finally, the United States has always been known for being a country of individuals. Americans are a people who march to the beat of their own drum, sometimes to the point where they make their own rules. We'll explore two notorious

American anti-heroes and how, despite being killers, they have achieved legendary status and are revered long after their deaths.

So, sit back, open the pages of this book, and be prepared to be intrigued, shocked, and edified. This is sure to be one of the most fascinating and engaging books of American biography you'll ever read!

THOMAS EDISON
INVENTING MODERN AMERICA

The fruits of the works of some of America's greatest heroes are with us every day, but we are rarely aware of them. I'm talking about some of the United States' greatest scientists, inventors, and doctors, who sacrificed their time—often for little monetary reward—to make their country and the world a better place.

These heroes may not have had the glamor of generals, statesmen, or entertainers, but their contributions to the country are just as, if not more, profound. And perhaps no American inventor/scientist has contributed more to our lives than Thomas Alva Edison (1847–1931).

Let's face it, without Edison's invention of the incandescent light bulb, our lives would be a whole lot different today and a whole lot darker! But it wasn't just the light bulb that Edison invented. The genius filed over 1,000 patents, most related to electricity, and included some of the following: the phonograph, a moving-picture projector, alkaline storage batteries, and an electric railroad train. If you think about it, without Edison, the modern electrical grid, and therefore the Computer/Internet Age, wouldn't have been possible.

But things weren't always easy for the self-taught scientist from Ohio.

A NOT SO GREAT START

Young Thomas Edison was always a creative dreamer, but that wasn't necessarily viewed as a good thing in mid-1800s America. His formal schooling was minimal and not of the best quality, with one of his teachers referring to him as *"a little addled"* when he was eight. A true genius like Edison didn't need school, though, especially in a system that stifled his creative abilities.

However, things weren't much better for him at home.

It would be an understatement to say that Edison's dad didn't understand him. He saw his son as a dreamer who wasted time with his experiments.

It wasn't until Edison found work as a telegraph operator in his twenties that he was able to properly work on his craft that would later make him famous. He also became a successful entrepreneur at an early age, starting a company in New Jersey.

The road to success wasn't always easy for Edison, though. Many of his inventions were never used or proved to be impractical. In 1875, he was cheated out of $275,000 by one of his business partners. Yet Edison displayed the true American spirit, learning from his setbacks and coming back even stronger each time.

LIGHTING UP AMERICA

His first major invention was the phonograph in 1877, which became the base for the record player and all later recording devices. The invention of the phonograph revolutionized the way people communicated because, prior to that, all correspondence and records were recorded by writing. Written documents are good, but they aren't always accurate. Edison's invention ensured that precise details of conversations, documents, and just about anything said could be accurately recorded.

Even more important than the invention of the phonograph, though, was Edison's invention of the incandescent light bulb.

It may not seem like a big deal, but this invention allowed electricity to illuminate homes and businesses for the first time. Before the light bulb, gas and oil were needed to light homes. Yet, as important as the invention of the incandescent light bulb is, Edison didn't come to it overnight in an *"aha"* moment. Instead, it was the result of a fairly long process with several detours and failures along the way.

Edison's initial experiments with a platinum filament were unsuccessful, until he began experimenting using a lower current through a copper wire with a carbon filament. After testing this new bulb, he discovered that that bulb would light indefinitely.

After perfecting the light bulb, Edison was then able to combine his scientific knowledge with his business acumen to make the consumption of electricity practical and inexpensive. Edison devised the country's first electrical power plant in New York City in 1882, which brought direct current (DC) to less than 100 people in the city. Within five years, those numbers had multiplied, and plans were being made to bring power to people throughout the country.

By 1886, though, Edison faced some new competition.

George Westinghouse, who, like Edison, was an engineer, inventor, and entrepreneur, also wanted to bring electrical power to America, but he had a different idea about how to do it. Instead of using direct current, Westinghouse planned to use alternating current (AC). AC power was potentially more dangerous than DC power because it used a higher voltage than DC. Westinghouse proposed using transformers to power down the voltage before the electricity was sent to homes.

SO BEGAN THE SO-CALLED *"WAR OF THE CURRENTS."*

Edison did whatever he could to keep AC power from growing in use, even supporting the use of the alternating current in the nation's first electric chair to demonstrate its lethality! In the end, AC proved to be much more efficient and Edison was pushed out of his own company, which became General Electric.

Edison didn't let the setback of losing the War of the Currents slow him down, though. During the 1890s, Edison and his growing team of scientists and engineers began experimenting in the nascent film industry. He was given a patent for a kinetoscope, which was an early type of motion picture viewer. Only one person could look through a particular kinetoscope at a time, so Edison had them installed in penny arcades and recreation destinations, such as the boardwalk of Atlantic City.

Ever the far-sighted entrepreneur, Edison then created a film studio in New Jersey to produce original short films for his kinetoscopes.

Another notable invention of Edison's was the rechargeable alkaline battery, in 1901. There were other batteries in existence before Edison's battery, but his battery was reusable and, perhaps most importantly, it was designed for the first electric cars!

Yes, you read that right: Edison's rechargeable battery was built specifically for electric cars. Long before the Volt and the Tesla, the Detroit Electric and the Baker Electric were electric cars that cruised around on America's streets and highways. For a while, it looked as though the electric car would be the future, with some of them able to go 100 miles or more on a single charge, but improvements in the internal combustion engine and the refinement of the assembly line gave victory to the gas guzzlers.

By the time Thomas Edison died, Americans already knew that he had impacted not just their country, but the entire world in profound ways. You could argue that Edison was the father of the 20th century and the world we live in today.

EDISON'S INFLUENCES ON EVERYDAY LIFE

Without Edison, things would be a whole lot darker, literally! A constant proponent of electrical power, even when the DC current lost to the AC current, Edison's spirit of competition helped create the modern electrical grid.

There would've been no Hollywood without Thomas Edison's efforts, either. Although Thomas Edison never intended—nor wanted—to be a flashy movie producer, the technology he invented, combined with his business skills, led to the creation of the American film industry.

Thomas Edison was truly an American original and an American hero. He was a genius ahead of his time, whose inventions and research on electricity has brought light and power to every corner of the globe. But perhaps what makes Edison truly an American hero was his ability to profit from those inventions. Yes, Edison believed in the purity of science and the idea of helping humanity advance, but he was also an entrepreneur with a keen business sense.

Edison was a self-made man who served as an example to Americans that, with some intelligence, ambition, resilience, and a few lucky breaks, the sky is the limit.

DID YOU KNOW?

- Edison was married twice. His first wife, Mary, died in 1884 at the age of 29. The couple had three children. Thomas married his second wife, Mina, in 1886. He had three more children with his second wife.

- Thomas and Mina's son Charles (1890–1969) had a fairly impressive and successful life himself. He ran his father's company until it was sold in 1957. He was also the Secretary of the Navy under President Roosevelt and was the Governor of New Jersey from 1941 to 1944.

- Thomas' son Theodore (1989–1992) carried on his father's success in the field of science. Theodore was a graduate of the prestigious Massachusetts Institute of Technology (MIT) and later developed several of his inventions.

- Edison's laboratory was in the Menlo Park section of Raritan Township, New Jersey. The name of the township was changed to Edison on November 10, 1954.

- Thomas Edison was often referred to as the *"Wizard of Menlo Park."*

WYATT EARP
TAMING THE WILD WEST

The United States may have been settled by European immigrants, but America developed a bit differently than Europe. One of the reasons for the United States' unique development was its big, wide-open frontier. From the earliest days of the settlers, Americans moved into the forests, valleys, plains, and mountains of the nation's Western frontier, which kept moving farther West as more immigrants came to settle it.

After the American Civil War, the Great Plains and the Intermountain West were the last true frontiers in America. California had become a state after the gold rush and the Mexican American War (1846–1848), but there was still plenty of open territory between the Golden State and Missouri.

It was wide-open territory with plenty of opportunities and also plenty of danger, which is why it became known as the Wild West.

In the late 1800s, there were many prospects for enterprising young men and women in the Western territories (most of the region had yet to be organized into states). The discovery of gold and silver deposits led to booms in mining and along with that growth came the construction of towns. Merchants were needed to supply the boomtowns with goods and, eventually, some more shady business ventures began cropping up across the West.

Gambling became popular, as did brothels and sex work. Although gambling and sex work were severely restricted or outlawed in most American states in the late 1800s, they were, for the most part, tolerated in the West.

But the reality was that the American West was a tough place. The towns were filled with a motley assortment of miners, cowboys, gamblers, ladies of the night, and various criminals trying to escape justice in the east.

Between the towns were seemingly endless stretches of mountains and plains, with an occasional Native American tribe—friendly or not—living off the land, as they had done for centuries.

It was the type of time and place that required lawmen who weren't afraid to get their hands dirty. The only type of lawmen who succeeded on the American frontier were those who were a little shady themselves.

Lawmen just like Wyatt Berry Stapp Earp, better known as Wyatt Earp.

Today, Wyatt Earp is best known for his part in the legendary shootout at the O.K. Corral in Tombstone, Arizona in 1881, but his life was so much more than that one event. Wyatt Earp blazed a sometimes violent but always interesting path across the American West with his six-shooter gun.

The complex Earp was a gambler turned criminal, turned lawman, turned buffalo hunter, turned lawman again. Earp was at the vanguard of the men and women who helped tame the West, bringing those once wild and lawless territories into the American Union.

INTERESTING ORIGINS

Earp was born on March 19, 1848 in the small town of Monmouth, Illinois. He had nine siblings, among whom were brothers Virgil and Morgan. Wyatt would later have many adventures with Virgil and Morgan, including the shootout at the O.K. Corral.

Wyatt's father was a veteran of the Mexican American War and a bit of a restless, free spirit. The Earp family moved quite a bit for people of their time, living in Pella, Iowa; San Bernardino, California; and finally, Lamar, Missouri.

As the Earp family moved across the West, young Wyatt eventually went out on his own to explore the world. He became interested in, and developed an acumen for, gambling and quickly learned that he needed to be tough in some of the hard-scrabble towns of the West.

Wyatt learned boxing and how to shoot a rifle and six-gun pistol, all of which later helped him survive in some pretty sticky situations.

After the Earp family moved to the southeastern Missouri town of Lamar in 1868, Wyatt got his first tastes of law enforcement, love, and living on the wrong side of the law.

The Earps moved to Lamar to farm and find other new opportunities, but those other opportunities quickly took precedence. Wyatt's father, Nicholas, became the town's constable, a title later passed to Wyatt.

Although crime wasn't much of a problem in sleepy Lamar, Wyatt excelled in his new job. He was said to be stern but fair and was well-liked by the people of the town. He was especially liked by a 20-year-old local woman named Urilla Sutherland.

Wyatt and Urilla embarked on a whirlwind courtship and married in 1870. The couple bought a new house and some land on the edge of town. They were about to welcome their first child when tragedy struck—Urilla died of typhoid fever while giving birth.

Wyatt was truly in love with Urilla, and her death sent him off the edge and into a very precarious chapter in his life. He began drinking heavily, was quick to fight, and started to engage in criminal activity. The details of his movements between 1870 and 1874 are a bit blurry, but a fairly colorful outline can be drawn.

A TURN TO CRIME

Wyatt was accused of embezzling money from the city of Lamar and, even worse, he was charged with horse theft in Native American Territory (present-day Oklahoma) in 1871.

Back in the Wild West, horse theft was one of the most serious offenses and was punishable by hanging in some jurisdictions. But Wyatt Earp was too crafty to let a horse thief charge be the end of him, so he escaped from the jail.

It should be pointed out that one didn't need to be a criminal mastermind to escape from a late 19th-century Western jail, but it still marked a steep change in his life.

THE LEGENDARY LAWMAN

For the next several months, it is believed that Earp drifted around the Great Plains, going from town to town, gambling, and generally avoiding criminal activity. When he wasn't gambling, Earp would hunt the ever-declining bison that still freely roamed the plains. Bison skins were worth nice sums of money, but Earp knew that it wouldn't be long before the herds were all but eliminated.

Earp also had an eternal traveling bone that needed to be exercised now and then.

It is believed that, while he was gambling and hunting bison on the Great Plains, Earp met a sex worker who suggested moving back east to Peoria, Illinois. The events after Earp's move back east are a bit cloudy. What is known, though, is that, in early 1872, Earp was arrested in a house of ill-repute with a sex worker named Sally Heckell. Not long after the arrest, the couple went back out West where Earp returned to law enforcement, earning his reputation as one of the greatest lawmen in American history.

Wyatt Earp was a handsome, yet slightly intimidating, man. At six feet, he was taller than most men of the time. His large, bushy handlebar mustache covered his mouth and expressions, and his steel-blue eyes were known to look right through a person. All of that was needed when Wyatt came to the tough town of Wichita, Kansas in 1874.

Wichita was a growing town in the 1870s, known for being a bit on the lawless side and filled with plenty of rowdy cowboys who traveled there with their herds before shipping them east on the railroads. Wichita, and most of Kansas, was policed by a cadre of marshals, but it was gambling and the sex trade that actually brought Wyatt to Kansas.

It turns out that Wyatt's brother, James, owned a brothel in Wichita and needed a little extra muscle keeping the rowdy cowboys in line. Wyatt was perfect for the job and quickly earned a reputation around the area as a fair but no-nonsense sort of guy. Success in Wichita brought him farther west to Dodge City, Kansas, where he met and befriended another legend of the Wild West, Doc Holliday. The two men were involved in several incidents in Dodge City, where Earp was forced to use violence and even kill some criminals in the course of making arrests.

Dodge City got so rowdy that Earp even banned people from openly carrying their guns!

Wyatt Earp truly was the long arm of the law in Dodge City and, by 1879, he had all but cleaned up the town. Crime and violence had dropped, and the old casinos and brothels were slowly being phased out. Earp had always walked a fine line between the law and the underworld, and towns that didn't have gambling or sex work just weren't the type of places he wanted to be. So, in 1879, he packed up and moved to southern Arizona to join his brother Virgil.

Virgil was the town constable in Prescott, Arizona, but it was profit-making that brought Wyatt to the area, especially the silver-rich town of Tombstone.

Tombstone, Arizona was aptly named. It was a rough locale that was controlled by local toughs, particularly a group known as the Outlaw Cowboys. The Cowboys were led by the Clanton brothers — Ike, Billy, and Phineas — with other notable members including Frank and Tom McLaury, Johnny Ringo, and Frank Stillwell. The Cowboys were essentially the mafia of their time and place: they robbed stagecoaches, rustled cattle, and extorted businesses, among other illegal activities.

Wyatt was later joined in Tombstone by his brothers Virgil and Jim and friend Doc Holliday. Wyatt worked in Tombstone as both a marshal and deputy sheriff, which put him squarely in the crosshairs of the Cowboys.

After the Earps and Holliday helped arrest a number of the Cowboys for stage-coach robberies, the two groups met on October 26, 1881 in a vacant lot known as the O.K. Corral on Fremont Street in Tombstone. At the time, Wyatt was no longer a cop and had instead been running local saloons, although his brother Virgil was the town marshal.

Virgil decided that the feud between the Earps and the Cowboys was going to end that day, one way or another.

When Virgil heard that Tom and Frank McLaury, Billy and Ike Clanton, and Billy Claiborne were hanging around the vacant lot, he deputized Wyatt, their brother Morgan, and Doc Holliday to disarm the crew of outlaws.

Needless to say, the Cowboys didn't give up their arms peacefully. As the two crews stood only six feet apart, someone—it is unknown who—started shooting. Within a couple of minutes, Virgil, Morgan, and Holliday were wounded and the McLaury Boys and Billy Clanton were dead.

The greatest gunfight in American history did not end there, though.

Ike Clanton had the gall to file murder charges against the Earps, but when the judge threw the charges out, he decided to get revenge. Virgil was shot in an ambush but lived. About four months later, Morgan was also ambushed and died.

Wyatt wasn't going to stand for that, especially since he and his brothers were planning on leaving Tombstone when the shootout happened. So, Wyatt did what he did best—he organized an even larger crew and hunted down as many of the Cowboys he could find. Wyatt and Doc Holliday eventually killed Jack Stillwell, Curly Bill Brocius, Johnny Barnes, and Florentino Cruz before calling it even and permanently leaving Tombstone.

Wyatt then traveled through the West some more, opening saloons, investing in mining operations, and even living in Nome, Alaska for a short time. He eventually retired and died in southern California in 1929 at the age of 80. Toward the end of his life, he became quite popular in Hollywood.

A LEGEND IN HIS OWN TIME

Wyatt Earp's status as an American hero and icon is truly legendary. Perhaps more than any other historical figure, Earp embodied the spirit of the Wild West and was the archetype for countless television and movie lawmen that were ubiquitous in the United States during the mid-20th century.

Earp was also the quintessential American success story: he fell a few times but got back up and was able to reinvent himself.

There is little doubt that, when it comes to American lawmen, Wyatt Earp is the first person who comes to most people's minds, and for good reason!

DID YOU KNOW?

- After Urilla died, Wyatt never again married, although he lived with three women as his common-law wives.

- Wyatt Earp had no known children.

- Part of the mystique of Wyatt Earp's life was the fact that he was never wounded in a gunfight.

- Wyatt was the referee for the well-publicized world title heavyweight boxing match between Bob Fitzsimmons and Tom Sharkey on December 2, 1896 in San Francisco, California. Because he was already well-known at the time, he was possibly the first celebrity to referee such a bout.

- Although Wyatt Earp was raised as a nominal Christian, his final common-law wife, Josephine Sarah Marcus, was Jewish. Because of her religion and Earp's lack of faith, his ashes were interred in a Jewish cemetery after he died in 1929.

ROBERT E. LEE
THE GENTLEMAN REBEL

You'll see throughout this book that the term *"hero"* is often very subjective. What one person may consider a hero might be considered a villain by someone else. Of course, this book is full of many Americans who are universally loved and respected by nearly every demographic in the United States, but there are a few who are a bit polarizing. With that said, the polarizing figures in this book are still considered heroes by large segments of the American population, and no matter what you may think of them, there is little doubt that they had significant impacts on American society and history.

The first of these polarizing heroes — anti-heroes if you will — is General Robert E. Lee.

Robert E. Lee was the Confederacy's best general in the American Civil War and, according to most historians, he was the most competent general on both sides of the war. There is little doubt that he was an important American military figure. However, it is still hard to overlook the fact that he took up arms against the United States and that he did so in support of slavery.

The reality is that Lee was far from being a black-and-white figure. He was politically against the Confederacy's secession from the Union, but as a loyal son of Virginia, went to war for his state and new country against his former country when called. Known as a consummate gentleman on and off the battlefield, he earned the respect of his foes as well as his men.

When the war was finally over, most in the North were willing to forgive General Lee and many even viewed him with a sense of admiration. In the decades after his death, he became a symbol of the Old South among southerners who resisted political and social change in their states.

Today, he is still held in high regard in many parts of the South, even as there are efforts to eliminate any public acknowledgment of his life.

So, let's take a look at General Robert E. Lee and see why he is still one of America's greatest heroes.

OVERCOMING HIS FATHER

Throughout this book, you'll see that nearly all of our great American heroes and heroines had to overcome numerous difficulties and challenges throughout their lives. As we've seen already, sometimes it was others' attitudes (Edison) and other times it was our heroes' personal demons (Earp). In Lee's case, it was his father.

Robert Edward Lee was born on January 19, 1807 on a plantation in northern Virginia to what would have normally been a privileged family. Both Robert's father, Henry, and his mother, Anne, came from aristocratic, slave-owning plantation families with generational wealth. The Lee family should have been able to rest on their financial laurels, but

Henry learned that, in the new country of America, wealth and privilege was something that could be gained *and* lost.

Henry Lee suffered a series of financial setbacks in the early 1800s, forcing his family to rely on the charity of their extended family. Henry eventually left the family in 1811, which meant that young Robert had to look elsewhere for male guidance.

Luckily, Anne Lee had some generous family members.

In the early 1800s, William Henry Fitzhugh was a very influential man in Virginia state politics and business. He was also the uncle of Robert E. Lee's future wife, Mary.

Fitzhugh saw great potential in the young Robert, who showed abundant academic promise. He made sure that Robert and his family had a good life and fine education and even arranged for Robert to attend the prestigious United States Military Academy in West Point, New York.

It was at West Point where Lee would make some lifelong relationships in the military and business. He would later serve and fight against some of those same men in the Civil War. Although Lee was known as being a friendly and fairly charismatic young man at West Point, he was more interested in his studies than having fun. When he wasn't drilling, training, or in class, Lee was buried in a book. He particularly excelled in math and science, but he did well in all his coursework, graduating second in his class in 1829.

Lee then did as many of the young military men of his generation did: he married, started a family, and was assigned to a post on what was then the Western frontier.

FIRST TASTE OF ACTION

Due to his high marks in school and acumen for science, Lee was assigned to be a military engineer. The work brought him to many different locations in less-developed parts of the United States, where he helped build bridges and do other construction that helped facilitate trade. It was rewarding work and Lee was quite successful, but like most men of his time, he wanted to prove himself on the battlefield.

He would get his chance in the Mexican American War (1846–1848).

Lee served as an officer under General Winfield Scott during the Mexican American War, seeing extensive action in Mexico in 1847. In particular, Lee was involved in the American landing at Veracruz that moved inland to Mexico City to strike the final blow against the Mexican Army. The war prepared Lee for the Civil War years later by allowing him to learn tactics in the field, make valuable professional connections, and establish his leadership abilities.

Always a student of men and ideas, Lee watched as Scott ordered successful cavalry attacks on the Mexicans, concluding that cavalry was the future of warfare in the 19th century. Lee also met and fought alongside many officers who were involved on both sides of the Civil War, including his primary adversary, Ulysses Grant.

But above all, in the Mexican American War, Lee established his intangible credentials as a leader. It was clear to all those below and above Lee's command that the young officer had the "X" factor that was needed to be a successful military leader in those days. He commanded and received respect, which only increased after he was wounded in battle.

Robert E. Lee became a true American hero during the Mexican American War, but just over ten years later, he became one of the country's most notorious rebels.

A RELUCTANT REBEL

It wasn't until the 1850s that Lee became a cavalry commander. After serving as superintendent of West Point for two years, he returned to the West to fight Native Americans in the mid- to late-1850s. However, by that point, it was obvious to most Americans that the nation was headed for a conflict that couldn't be avoided. Lee was personally against secession and, although he did own a few slaves throughout his lifetime, he was never a large slave owner. For the most part, he was like any other Southerner of his class during the period.

But no matter how much he may have tried to avoid the coming Civil War, the forces were too big, even for a man like Robert E. Lee. His first major foray into the coming conflict was when he was ordered to put down John Brown's attempted uprising at Harpers Ferry, Virginia in October 1859. He did his duty in doing so but knew that more conflicts were yet to come.

Lee was stationed in Texas when the Civil War began, but instead of joining the Confederacy right away, he returned to Washington. Lee initially accepted a promotion to colonel in the U.S. cavalry and was even later offered the rank of general, but when Virginia seceded in May 1861, his role in American history was all but assured. He immediately resigned from the United States Army and, although he initially intended to remain neutral, he joined the military of Virginia.

The Confederate Army then made him one of their first generals and in little time he was commanding the whole show.

By all accounts, it was a role he didn't immediately relish. He didn't want to fight against his country, but at the same time, he knew he couldn't fight against his state. Lee also knew that the South was materially overmatched. While many Southerners, even several Confederate political and military leaders, believed that they would win the war quickly, Lee knew that wasn't the case. The pragmatic Lee understood that the South's best hope was to win some impressive victories, thereby forcing the U.S. to either recognize the Confederacy or to allow the Southern states to rejoin the Union under good terms.

But for that to happen, Lee would have to pull off some incredible magic.

THE HERO OF THE SOUTH

General Lee was always a numbers guy, even when he was a child and, after looking at the numbers of the Union versus the Confederacy, he knew that things didn't look good. The North had about 20 million people and growing when the war began, compared to about 9 million for the South, of which about 3.5 million were slaves. To make matters more difficult for the South, the North was being fed by a constant stream of immigrants from Ireland, Scandinavia, and the German-speaking kingdoms. All of those countries contributed to filling the ranks of the Union's many ethnic regiments.

Lee fought entirely in the Eastern Theater of the Civil War, working his way up the ranks after early victories in the Seven Days Battle to become the Commander of the Army of Northern Virginia in June 1862.

Riding on his trusty horse, Traveller, Lee inspired confidence in his troops, regardless of their rank, pushing them to keep fighting, often against great odds.

Lee had to take many gambles to keep the Confederacy in the war. His biggest gamble was invading the North in the Gettysburg Campaign during the summer of 1863. Although that gamble didn't pay off with a Confederate victory, it earned Lee the title of General-in-Chief of the Confederate forces in February 1865.

But it was a title he didn't hold for long. On April 9, 1865, after losing the Battle of Appomattox to General Grant, Lee surrendered to the Union Army. It marked the end of the war and the military career of General Lee.

After the war, Lee found that there was little for him to return to or to do. He was stripped of his citizenship and his family's land was seized by the government and turned into Arlington National Cemetery. He took an oath of allegiance to the United States, but his citizenship was not restored. Lee then led a rather unassuming life, teaching at and becoming president of Washington College in Lexington, Virginia until he died of heart disease on October 12, 1870.

Although Robert E. Lee's life ended rather inauspiciously, his impact on American history is profound. He led the Confederate Army to numerous battlefield victories and was close to giving the Confederacy victory on more than one occasion. His battlefield tactics were studied for decades by later generals; even modern generals and military leaders still point to him as being one of the best tacticians and leaders America has ever produced.

But the fact that he rebelled against America on behalf of a government that supported slavery is something that many can't forget.

Still, Robert E. Lee has been viewed as a hero by large segments of the American population since he first rode on Traveller into battle. President Gerald Ford restored his citizenship in 1975, the main characters in the hit 1980s American television show *The Dukes of Hazzard* had his name emblazoned on their signature hot rod, and his statues and monuments still stand across the South, all proving that General Robert E. Lee is a true American hero to many.

DID YOU KNOW?

- After the war, Lee was a proponent of the Lost Cause movement. The Lost Cause movement argued that the South was essentially the victim of Northern aggression.

- Robert and Mary had three sons: Custis, Robert Junior, and William.

- Lee acquired a few different nicknames in his lifetime, including the Virginia Gentleman, Granny Lee, and the Great Tycoon. He was given the Granny Lee nickname due to his cautious movements early in the Civil War, but once he became successful that name quickly faded.

- Although Lee avoided politics for the most part after the war, he was vocal about his opposition to the Radical Republicans and their plans for Reconstruction.

- His body was interred under the chapel at Washington College. The College was later renamed Washington *and* Lee University in commemoration of Lee.

UPTON SINCLAIR
THE AMERICAN CONSUMER'S FIRST HERO

Despite their different backgrounds and the periods in which they lived, all of the great heroes in this book have one thing in common—they fought a great fight, often against great odds. Whether the fight was against attitudes in society, an enemy army, or laws deemed unjust, the heroes in this book stood by what they believed in, sometimes at great risk to their livelihoods and lives. Some of the heroes used guns and other weapons to fight their battles, while others followed the adage that the *"pen is mightier than the sword."*

American author Upton Sinclair is one such hero who followed that aphorism.

Long before famed consumer advocate Ralph Nader railed against corporate corruption and the dangers that the American public faced due to malfeasance in big business, Upton Sinclair wrote gripping, graphic novels that exposed the lurid underbelly of factory and labor life in America. Best known for his 1906 novel *The Jungle,* Sinclair wrote over 100 books and short stories that chronicled the best—and worst— of life in America in the late 1800s and early 1900s—a period known as the Progressive Era.

Thanks to Sinclair's books, there are standards and restrictions on what can be put in our food as well as how it is packaged and prepared. Sinclair's works also led to strict safety requirements on job sites, opening the way for a more mainstream labor movement in America.

THE HAVES AND THE HAVE NOTS

Upton Beall Sinclair Junior was born on September 20, 1878 in Baltimore, Maryland to Upton Sinclair Senior and Priscilla Sinclair. He experienced early hardships, as his family had to relocate often due to his father's unsteady employment. Upton Senior was also an alcoholic, which contributed to the family's chronic poverty.

But wealth and privilege were never far from young Upton.

As his family struggled to make ends meet, his mother's family, the Hardens, were an old, established east coast WASP family. Upton would spend summers and vacations with members of the Harden family. Although he was treated quite well by them, he knew that they were truly from a different world. His relatives from the Harden family lived in big homes, had servants, and were among the first people in their areas to own cars. This early contrast in lifestyles formed the basis for how Upton Sinclair viewed the world and was an overarching theme in many of his books and short stories. To Upton Sinclair, the America he knew was a great place, but it was also a country of haves and have nots.

While he was in his early teens, Upton discovered that he had a talent for writing. Although he struggled in school with the hard sciences, Upton was a true wordsmith from an early age.

He wrote short stories, dime-store books, and jokes for any magazine that would buy them, becoming successful enough to support himself and his parents while he was still a teenager.

He briefly attended the prestigious Columbia University in New York City, but its curriculum was too restrictive for the young Sinclair. He knew what he wanted to do in life—save America through his writings—so there was little need for him to continue.

Instead, he moved to Chicago to research and write his most important book.

THE JUNGLE

In 1904, Sinclair came up with an idea for a book that would forever change his life and how business was done in the United States. An ardent socialist at the time, the idealistic Sinclair wanted to advance his beliefs by showing the world just how corrupt and dangerous big business had become in America. So, to conduct his experiment, Sinclair decided to travel to the heart of America: Chicago, Illinois.

After getting a job in one of Chicago's many meatpacking factories, he saw just how desperate things were. The primarily foreign labor force had few options and often found it difficult to communicate with their bosses or each other. Accidents, sometimes resulting in death, were fairly common on the factory floors and there was no recompense if a worker was unfortunate enough to get injured.

The workers also had to work long hours, were paid truly little, and were often subject to exploitation by their bosses.

And forget about retirement plans, pensions, or 401(K)s; workers in the meatpacking plants often felt lucky just to live long enough to spend their meager paychecks!

And as bad as the conditions were for the workers, the condition of the food being made was even worse.

The factories were filled with rats that would urinate and defecate in the meat. They would also often get caught in the meat right before it was packaged!

Nothing like a bit of rat with your hamburger, right?

Needless to say, few health and safety guidelines regulated how the meat was packaged or the type of condition in which it was allowed to hit the shelves. Rancid meat was common, and people routinely got sick and died from tainted meat packaged in these factories.

When *The Jungle* was first published in serialized form in 1905 in the socialist newspaper, *Appeal to Reason*, it was quite a sensation. It was a subject that every American cared about, regardless of his or her political affiliation. Americans who would never dream of purchasing a socialist newspaper were suddenly looking through newsstands for *Appeal to Reason* so they could read *The Jungle*. Due to its popularity, *The Jungle* was published as a book by Doubleday in 1906 and quickly became a bestseller.

The success of *The Jungle* brought fame and success to Upton Sinclair but, more importantly in his eyes, it changed the way business was done in America.

New laws and agencies to oversee how food was processed, handled, and packaged were quickly established. The Federal Meat Inspection Act became law in 1906 and the Pure Food and Drug Act followed later that same year. The Pure Food and Drug Act became the basis for the Food and Drug Administration, which was formed in 1930.

Few could argue that one book has had a bigger impact on American history, but Sinclair was only getting started.

CONTINUING HIS CRUSADE

The success of *The Jungle* gave Sinclair the economic freedom and notoriety to concentrate on his big picture message of social change. He unsuccessfully ran for governor of California, started a utopian community, and became more involved in the early Socialist Party. Sinclair also continued to write, both fiction books with a message and non-fiction articles and essays.

The next major novel Sinclair published was the 1917 book, *King Coal*. Although not as sensational or as graphic as *The Jungle*, *King Coal* accurately depicted the plight of mine workers across America. Theirs was one of the most vital, yet dangerous, jobs in the country, but their bosses cared more about their equipment. The unions that were supposed to protect the mine workers were often little better than the company owners.

Sinclair continued to write and offer his ideas on American society until he died on November 25, 1968 at the age of 90.

Although there may be American writers who are better known and have been more commercially successful than Upton Sinclair, few — or none — have had the same impact on American society. Upton Sinclair raised the alarm on abuses that the working class was being subjected to and made it known that Americans were eating food contaminated by vermin. Because of his efforts, great changes were undertaken that made working conditions and the food we eat safer. Sinclair's efforts later influenced and inspired other labor and consumer rights activists, such as Ralph Nader, and for that alone he should be considered a true American hero.

DID YOU KNOW?

- Sinclair was married three times. He divorced his first wife, Meta, in 1911. His second wife, Mary, died in 1961 and his third wife, Mary, died in 1967, a year before he died.

- Sinclair had a son, David, with his first wife. He had no other children.

- Upton unsuccessfully ran several times for political office in California. Since he ran on the Socialist Party ticket, he received little financial support and was generally eschewed by the public, who equated socialism with communism in the 1920s. His best showing was when he ran as a Democrat for California governor in 1934, although he lost that race by nearly 300,000 votes.

- The 2007 film *There Will Be Blood* was an adaption of his 1927 novel *Oil!* Perhaps somewhat surprising is that, so far, the only film adaptation of *The Jungle* was a 1914 silent film.

- Sinclair was a health fanatic for most of his life, following strict diets and never drinking very much. He attributed his life of good health and longevity to his diet.

HELEN KELLER
AMERICA'S HEROINE OF PEOPLE WITH DISABILITIES

Most of us are blessed enough to have the ability to see and hear. Losing either one of these senses would be incredibly tragic, painful, and difficult. It would require learning how to speak with our hands, to read lips, or to read brail. The process would be long and arduous, and you would no doubt at times feel like giving up; but thankfully, the process, and professionals who know it, would be there to help.

Can you imagine becoming deaf or blind and not having the process or professionals to help you? Worse yet, can you even imagine what it would be like to be deaf *and* blind?

That was exactly the reality Helen Keller faced after she lost her hearing and sight at 19 months old in 1882. Considering the time, most thought that the best the girl could hope for was to end up in a comfortable sanitarium, away from the general public. For a time, it looked like that was what would happen to Helen.

But with plenty of sheer will and the help of a friend, Helen Keller was able to live with her disabilities. She would go on to be a tireless advocate for deaf and blind people, helping establish organizations that assist people with those disabilities. Today, Helen Keller is rightfully considered one of America's foremost champions of disabled people, with her legacy being seen and felt throughout the country in many ways.

After all, it was Helen Keller who paved the way for the acceptance of people with disabilities in mainstream society. You could argue that, without her efforts, there would never have been an Americans with Disabilities Act or any legal protections for disabled people.

DEALT A LOSING HAND?

People routinely fall on bad luck and are dealt bad hands throughout their lives. There is no need to list what kind of misfortunes we can all face, but I think it would be pretty safe to say that losing your sight and hearing before the age of two can be about the worst luck one can think of. For Helen Keller, though, it eventually turned out to be a winning hand.

The first few years of Helen's life were certainly difficult: she struggled to communicate with her family, although she was able to do so with a rudimentary form of sign language. Eventually, her parents, who were from influential and relatively well-off families in northern Alabama, contacted another great American hero — Alexander Graham Bell.

You see, Bell, who is known for his experiments and inventions concerning sound, was working with deaf children. Although Bell never personally worked with Helen, he put the Keller family in contact with the Perkins School for the Blind in Boston, Massachusetts.

Of course, Helen was not only blind, she was also deaf, which made hers an especially difficult case. After the Kellers worked out the financial arrangements with the school, a 20-year-old woman named Anne Sullivan was sent to the Keller home to teach Helen to communicate. Sullivan was herself partially blind, so she had personal experience with one of Helen's disabilities, but she would have to work hard to help the little girl live with both her disabilities.

Needless to say, the process wasn't easy. You have to remember that, when Helen lost her sight and hearing, she wasn't even two years old, which meant that she wasn't self-aware. Helen Keller had yet to speak properly and had no real concept of the world when she became deaf and blind.

So, Sullivan began by placing objects in one of Helen's hands and then writing their name on her other hand. After about a year of exclusively working with Sullivan, Helen was ready for formal schooling. She first attended the Perkins Institute for the Blind, where she learned how to read in braille. Helen could then learn from others to a certain degree, but she still had to learn how to communicate.

Keller and Sullivan moved to New York City in 1894, where Helen attended schools for the deaf. Keller refined her rudimentary signing into a sign language that others could understand. Incredibly, Keller also began learning how to speak at this point in her life. She could read sign language with her hands, and for those who didn't know sign language, she would place her hands on their lips, thereby reading their speech.

By 1896, Helen Keller was ready to fully integrate herself into the world of the hearing and sighted.

AN INCREDIBLE WOMAN

Helen Keller's incredible battle to live with her disabilities began to garner media attention in the late 1800s and early 1900s. Famous American writer Samuel Clemens/Mark Twain became an admirer and friend of Keller. He respected the young woman's tenacity, ambition, and intelligence and did whatever he could to support her.

Clemens introduced Keller to influential, old money type people around Boston who gave her financial support and helped her gain admittance to Radcliffe College in Cambridge, Massachusetts in 1900. Radcliffe was the female, sister institution to Harvard University before the two institutions merged.

Helen defied all odds by graduating cum laude in 1904, becoming the first deafblind person to hold a college degree. It was certainly quite an accomplishment, but Helen still had plenty of work to do in her life.

She practiced her speech for hours every day. It didn't take long for her hard work to pay off, as she was offered speaking engagements around the country in the 1910s. No doubt many people who came to see her thought of her as a bit of a novelty — possibly even a sideshow type of attraction — but everyone was moved by her speeches.

Helen Keller was quite loquacious: her vocabulary was expansive, and it was hard to tell that she was deaf. Many people may have gone to see Helen Keller speak, thinking of her as a curiosity, but nearly all left with a greater understanding of disability. Before long, Helen recognized her innate power to move people, which she used to advocate for deaf and blind people.

Keller traveled around the U.S. and the world extensively in the 1920s, relentlessly advocating for deaf and blind people and all people with disabilities. Although she was one of the first true advocates for people with disabilities in America, she came on the scene at the right time. As we discussed with Upton Sinclair, the United States was changing tremendously in the early 1900s: laws were being enacted to protect workers and consumers and there was a general attitude that the government could be used to make Americans' lives better. Helen Keller found her place in the wider Progressive Movement, becoming a member of the Socialist Party but never denouncing her strong Christian beliefs.

UNDENIABLE INFLUENCE

Helen Keller wrote a bestseller about her early life, *The Story of My Life*, and a philosophical treatise titled *My Religion*. She was always eager to learn, until she died at the age of 87 on June 1, 1968.

Among all the heroes and heroines profiled in this book, Helen Keller is arguably the most inspiring. Many people in her situation would've simply given up. There are times when Keller also wanted to quit.

But she persevered and lived with her disabilities, actually proving that some of the toughest roadblocks and barriers in life are just challenges waiting to be met. Helen Keller devoted her life to integrating people with disabilities into mainstream society and helping them rise above their perceived limitations.

Helen Keller was a humble woman, and she may have

objected to being called a heroine. But there is little doubt that, when anyone compiles a list of the greatest American heroes and heroines, she has to be somewhere near the top.

DID YOU KNOW?

- Helen Keller never married and had no children. She was involved in a serious relationship with a man named Peter Fagan in the 1910s. Due to social norms of the time that said people with disabilities shouldn't be involved in romantic/sexual relationships, Keller's family, and even Anne Sullivan, successfully discouraged this and any future relationships of Helen's.

- After Anne Sullivan died in 1936, a Scottish woman named Polly Thomson was hired to be Helen's helper; by that time, though, she needed little help.

- Although Helen Keller lived the majority of her life away from Alabama, the state takes great pride in her being a native daughter. A hospital in Alabama is named for her and, in 2003, she was depicted on a U.S. quarter that commemorated Alabama's statehood.

- Helen Keller's early life story, based largely on her autobiography, was turned into a live drama titled *The Miracle Worker* in the 1950s. The stage act was later produced for film and television.

- The nickname Miracle Worker was given to Keller by Samuel Clemens.

BOOKER T. WASHINGTON
FROM SLAVE TO SUCCESS

Many of the heroes in this book were placed in seemingly impossible situations out of their control. We've already seen how Helen Keller faced what most people would've thought to be insurmountable physical disabilities, but due to her will to live, she prospered. Some limitations outside of a person's control, though, are the result of society.

The world we live in today is quite different than the world 100 years ago. Just over 100 years ago, the United States was emerging from the Civil War and the legacy of slavery, with racial segregation the rule of the land throughout much of the South. There were few opportunities for Black Americans in the South—or poor Whites, for that matter. So, for a person born into slavery to become a successful, world-famous philanthropist and entrepreneur was truly incredible.

But that is exactly what Booker Taliaferro Washington did.

Going from slavery to even more uncertainty as a former slave with no formal education, Booker T. Washington embarked on an odyssey that brought him from slavery to social and financial success. While on his incredible journey, Washington met more than one American president, and even visited the White House, long before Black Americans were allowed to do such a thing. But the influence Washington gained and the respect he commanded was such that Americans from all backgrounds listened to what the man from Tuskegee had to say.

By the time Booker T. Washington died at the relatively young age of 59 in 1915, he had done more to help Black Americans than most other leaders before or after him combined. He helped former slaves and their descendants learn valuable job and social skills and to generally be independent and self-sufficient.

For those reasons alone, Booker T. Washington is an American hero.

NO ONE SAID LIFE WAS EASY

Booker was born into slavery on April 5, 1856 to a Virginia slave named Jane. His father is believed to have been a White man, although his details and background were never revealed. Jane gave her son the name Booker Taliaferro (the family name of her owner), and young Booker later took the name of his stepfather, Washington Ferguson, as his surname and kept Taliaferro as his middle name.

The choice of names may seem like a minor detail of an extraordinary person's life, but it perfectly encapsulates Booker T. Washington's life-long attitude and philosophy. He never held grudges and never lived in the past. To Washington, there was no sense in going through life angry over things he couldn't control or change. Instead, he focused all of his energy on bettering himself.

Booker learned at an early age that, no matter how bad things may have been in the past, they could always be better, or worse!

When the Civil War ended in 1865, Booker became one of the four million slaves who were emancipated. However, the Washington family's victory over slavery proved to be somewhat short-lived. Making a living proved to be difficult in West Virginia, where they had to compete with a larger White population that was often just as poor.

Booker had to work in dangerous jobs at an early age, such as in mines and salt furnaces, just to help his family make ends meet. But Booker always knew there was more to the world than just getting by; he wanted to know what was out there and, if possible, to help other people in his situation.

With the help of kindly community patrons, Booker began learning how to read and attended school in West Virginia. Once he learned how to read, he read whatever he could. Eventually, he came across some literature for the Hampton Institute. The Hampton Institute, located in Hampton, Virginia, was one of the early Historical Black Colleges and Universities (HBCUs) in the United States.

The Hampton Institute was founded in 1868 by philanthropists as a private university for freedmen (former slaves). The emphasis was initially on vocational skills that were intended to help former slaves become self-sufficient.

Booker saved what little money he had and began the more than 400-mile trip from Malden, West Virginia to Hampton, Virginia in 1872 at the age of 16. Today, the trip would take several hours by car, but Booker had to stop along the way to make money doing odd jobs.

He left home by stagecoach, but also traveled many miles by foot. He would sweep floors of businesses during the day and sleep under wooden sidewalks at night. When he finally made it to the Hampton Institute, it was everything he thought it would be.

But once more, Washington faced adversity.

When Washington finally arrived at the Hampton Institute, he was broke, dirty, and hungry, but not broken. Perhaps owing to his appearance and that he did not have money to pay for tuition, young Washington was passed over for admission in favor of several other students.

He was finally given a chance when the schoolmistress asked him to sweep a floor, to prove that he would work for his education. He cleaned it so thoroughly that the teacher could not find a speck of dirt—he had passed his entrance exam! They gave him a paid janitor position, which helped pay for his tuition.

Washington was impressed with the school's orderliness and emphasis on practical, vocational education. Although Washington believed that learning history and the humanities were important, he believed that Black Americans in the late 1800s and early 1900s were better served to learn about business and acquiring job skills than learning Greek or Latin.

Washington became one of Hampton's top students and in no time was tutoring and then teaching. He graduated from Hampton and then studied at Wayland Seminary in Washington, D.C., before he was offered the position that would change his—and countless other people's—life: President of the Tuskegee Normal and Industrial Institute in Tuskegee, Alabama.

By 1881, when Washington began his grand experiment at Tuskegee, it was clear to many Americans, Black and White, that Booker T. Washington was a man who was going to make a difference in the country. He was smart, ambitious, and had inherent leadership skills that couldn't be denied.

A NEW KIND OF LEADER

When Washington arrived in Tuskegee, he was more than able to apply what he had learned at Hampton. Besides the general knowledge he gained from Hampton and Wayland, Washington continued to make inroads with White philanthropists around the country. These wealthy benefactors would be crucial to the Tuskegee Institute's survival and eventual success.

When Washington arrived in Alabama, he wasn't impressed, to say the least.

The school consisted of only one building but there were hundreds of students who wanted to enroll. The always industrious Washington looked at the problem as a lesson to be overcome and the first chance to make his philosophy a reality.

After buying 100 acres of land, Washington had the students and faculty begin working together to build new lecture halls, dormitories, and other buildings for the campus. The students cut the wood, made the bricks, and then constructed all of the buildings themselves. It would be their first lesson in self-sufficiency.

But it is expensive to operate a college/university, and since Tuskegee was a private college, it relied on the largesse of wealthy benefactors. Since the Black community had only recently been freed from slavery, few had the money to contribute, especially in the South, so Booker had to appeal to Whites as well.

Washington's oratory skills were excellent. He was engaging, yet approachable and down to earth. Organizations across the United States — and later the world — paid Washington to speak to them about the progress of Black America and what the future might hold.

All of his speeches were well-received by spectators and the press, which eventually culminated in him giving an address on September 18, 1895, at the Cotton States and International Exposition.

In the speech, Washington conceded political power in the Southern states to the Whites on the condition that Blacks would be given education and legal protection. Some Black leaders of the time considered it a surrender and termed it the Atlanta Compromise, while others believe it was the best, most pragmatic course at the time.

Washington believed that pragmatism was required, whether in education or politics. He believed it was his mission to train former slaves and their children for a time when they would have more rights and — eventually — political power.

And there is little doubt for historians that Washington's approach had success.

Enrollment in the Tuskegee Institute increased annually and, before long, other HBCUs were following the institute's template by advocating vocational skills as the core of their curricula. Slowly but surely, Black-owned businesses began cropping up across the South and Black farmers were becoming more and more successful.

For Washington, who was never much for personal glory, the highlight of his career came when he dined at the White House with President Theodore Roosevelt in 1901. Although this is no big deal today, Washington was the first Black person to have an official dinner with the president. It was certainly a sign of the changing times.

A LASTING LEGACY

Booker T. Washington's image has gone through transformations in the 100 years since his death. As Black leaders pushed hard for civil rights in the 1950s and 60s, and some such as Malcolm X and the Black Panthers even advocated violence, Washington began to be seen as too accommodating of the segregated political system. But more recently that has changed.

Historians now recognize that, without the efforts of Booker T. Washington, Black America may not have been in a position to advocate anything in the 50s and 60s. Washington generally uplifted a people who had been enslaved less than a generation earlier by teaching them the importance of education and self-reliance.

We often make our modern society much more complex than it needs to be. We tend to overthink and overanalyze every little problem; often, these aren't problems in the first place. Booker T. Washington is a hero from a time in America that was much simpler than today. It wasn't necessarily a better place or time, but it was one where a pragmatic person with an incredible will, like Washington, could forge a path to tackle some pretty big, long-term issues. Rome wasn't built in a day and big problems are never solved overnight.

DID YOU KNOW?

- Booker was married three times. His first two wives, Fannie and Olivia, preceded him in death, while his third wife, Margaret, lived until 1925.

- As Washington traveled to raise money for the Tuskegee Institute, he met and befriended some pretty famous and influential people. He shared the stage with Mark Twain/Samuel Clemens and received financial support from George Eastman of the Eastman Kodak Company and Julius Rosenwald of Sears, Roebuck and Company.

- Washington died of complications from high blood pressure on November 14, 1915. He had collapsed while visiting New York City for business. After doctors gave him a grim prognosis, he boarded a train to Tuskegee, Alabama, where he died within hours of his arrival.

- Booker's best-known literary work is his 1901 autobiography, *Up from Slavery*. The book is known for being extremely optimistic in tone, despite the often somber historical circumstances.

- Although W. E. B. Du Bois is often portrayed as Washington's primary critic within the Black community, the two men collaborated on more than one project, including the 1907 book *The Negro in the South*.

LEWIS AND CLARK
THE FIRST AMERICAN EXPLORERS

We've already discussed how America was settled by brave pioneers and explorers. These men and women were willing to move to the untamed Western frontier and live without services, sometimes among Native American tribes defending their land.

Any small illness or disease could lead to death and anyone who took the risk of embarking on this type of life had to be truly self-sufficient. But before what we know today as the West could ever be settled and farmed, it had to become part of the United States.

The big opportunity for American expansion came in 1803. The French dictator Napoleon was constantly fighting nearly every other country in Europe, so to pay for his wars, he sold most of France's possessions in North America to President Thomas Jefferson and the United States for $15,000,000.

Yes, that is a fair chunk of change even today, so you can just imagine what the sale was like at the time. It got America 823,000 square miles of land, which included everything west of the Mississippi River, north of the Red River of the South, and into the Rocky Mountains.

This purchase became known as the Louisiana Purchase.

The purchase was a politically risky move for Jefferson, who had a difficult time justifying the cost. He knew that he could only do so if the benefits of the purchase could be demonstrated. To do that, Jefferson needed to send men into that great unknown territory.

The task eventually went to Meriwether Lewis and William Clark. Although these are two great American heroes, their contribution to American history can only be considered together. For two years, from May 1804 to September 1806, Lewis and Clark led an expedition that trekked from near present-day St. Louis, Missouri to the Pacific Ocean and back.

Along the way, they had some great adventures, met many interesting people, and—above all—laid American claim to much of the area that would later become the western United States.

There have been other great American explorers since Lewis and Clark, but none had a greater impact on American history, which is why Lewis and Clark are among America's greatest heroes.

TWO UNLIKELY PARTNERS

Before the Lewis and Clark expedition could get underway and make those two men American heroes, the idea had to be thought of and then put into motion. Although the U.S. government of 1803 was far less bureaucratic than it is today, President Jefferson still had to get through a couple of layers of red tape.

The idea came to Jefferson after Scottish explorer Alexander Mackenzie trekked across most of what is today Canada, sighting the Pacific Ocean in 1793. Jefferson wanted to do the same with the newly purchased Louisiana Territory, but he had to overcome some political foes within his government. Portraying the expedition as a scientific venture, Jefferson got $2,324 for the project, which he named the Corps of Discovery.

Jefferson selected the group's leader, Meriwether Lewis, who then chose William Clark as his second-in-command. It turned out to be an excellent match, but in many ways, the two were an unlikely duo.

Lewis was born in 1774 in the Colony of Virginia, although he grew up in Georgia. Like many boys of that era who were not in the upper class, Meriwether wasn't formally educated until he was a teenager.

But that didn't mean he wasn't educated.

Young Meriwether spent a lot of time in the woods, hunting, hiking, and learning about the flora and fauna of America. Always an inquisitive young man, he read about his discoveries when he could and also became acquainted with members of the Cherokee Indian tribe. His Cherokee friends taught him even more about the plants and animals he encountered, as well as some of the traditions and norms of indigenous peoples.

Although the Lewis family was not very wealthy, they were connected to some influential people in Virginia society. After receiving a formal education in his teens, Meriwether entered the military.

Due to a combination of his connections and his intelligence, he rose to the rank of captain. Meriwether was unlike many of the other officers and sometimes had a hard time fitting in with them. He was a good officer and not afraid of battle, but he was always more interested in reading and pondering the mysteries of life.

The inquisitive young military officer came to the attention of fellow Virginian, President Thomas Jefferson, who assigned him as Secretary to the President in 1801.

The two men spent much of Jefferson's presidency at Monticello, pouring through the books about North American geography, botany, and biology in Jefferson's voluminous library. When Jefferson announced the formation of the Corps of Discovery, there was no doubt in his mind that Meriwether Lewis would lead the expedition.

Meriwether didn't have to search long or far to find his right-hand man. William Clark was born in 1770 in Virginia and, like Lewis, was schooled by a combination of tutors and the great outdoors. Although both men embodied the true American pioneer spirit, their lives before the expedition took slightly different paths.

Clark was raised primarily in Kentucky, which in the late 1700s was truly the Western frontier. Although he was literate, Clark was far from being the bookworm that Lewis was. Instead of spending his free time reading, young William preferred to roam the woods around what is today Louisville, hunting, fishing, and camping.

Clark met Lewis when both were in the military but, unlike Lewis, Clark saw extensive combat in the Northwest Indian War (1785–1795). It was during that war when Clark's somewhat complex views on American Indians were formed.

He had true respect for all of the Native American tribes, yet he believed in American expansion, at the expense of those tribes if necessary.

So, when Lewis was given the command of the expedition, he knew that there was no better man to back him up than the backwoods Native American fighter Clark.

AN INCREDIBLE JOURNEY

When Lewis and Clark began their journey down the Ohio River from Pittsburgh, Pennsylvania on August 31, 1803, they had a fairly well-laid out plan for their mission.

The expedition's mission was multi-faceted: part scientific, part political, and part economic.

They were to document the flora and fauna of the Louisiana Territory as they traveled. This was Lewis's strongpoint. He meticulously cataloged all of the plants and animals they found, detailing which were edible and useful for future human settlement.

The overarching goal of the mission was to find a river route to the Pacific Ocean before the Europeans did and, along the way, map the territory for future expeditions and settlement.

The cultural and economic goals of the expedition coincided. Lewis and Clark were to contact the Native American tribes, report their numbers back to the government, and determine which were suitable for trade. This part of the mission was primarily handled by Clark.

Their route followed the Missouri River and, before too long, the two men and their small cadre of companions found themselves in a completely different world. The snow and cold of the Great Plains were like nothing they'd ever experienced and the Sioux tribe of what is today the Dakotas were much more fearsome and warlike than the eastern Native American tribes.

By the time they got to what is today Bismarck, North Dakota in the winter of 1804–1805, things were starting to look pretty grim. Lewis and Clark found themselves in the middle of a war between the Sioux and Omaha tribes and, to make matters worse, the Spanish sent an expedition to find and, possibly, kill them.

The two explorers had few options. Due to the harsh winters of the upper Great Plains, they were forced to stay in their camp for months. They only had about 40 men to fight off any attack from the Sioux.

But Lewis and Clark rose to the occasion by displaying superb leadership skills.

Their dilemma in Dakota territory was solved by a combination of bravery, intelligence, and diplomacy. They gave gifts to the Sioux leaders and welcomed a new and useful pair into their expedition: a Shoshone Indian woman named Sacagawea and her French explorer husband Toussaint Charbonneau. The pair knew enough English and regional indigenous languages to act as their interpreters for the remainder of the trip.

Lewis and Clark also learned that Clark's slave, York, was an asset on the expedition.

Since no American Indians had seen a Black man before that point, York was a bit of a curiosity to many of the tribes the expedition encountered. Many of them thought he resembled a bear and, since bears are sacred to many of the tribes, York was also believed to be imbued with mystical powers.

Needless to say, Lewis and Clark used York to their advantage whenever possible.

When the expedition finally got to the Pacific in the winter of 1805–1806, the two explorers had to make some more important decisions. They pitched camp north of the Columbia River, but were ravaged by winter conditions, a lack of food, and influenza. Morale was low, so Lewis and Clark allowed all members of the expedition — including Sacagawea and York — to vote on staying or leaving. The group voted to move south of the Columbia River, which perhaps saved all of them.

On the return journey, the expedition faced Native American tribes even more intent on defending their land. They had some of their horses stolen and Clark was even shot by friendly fire, but they eventually made it home.

When Lewis and Clark gave their report of the momentous journey to President Jefferson, they were thanked for their service and offered nice government posts but received little fanfare by the press or the public.

Lewis and Clark wouldn't become heroes until well into the 1800s.

THE TRUE IMPACT OF LEWIS AND CLARK

The impact of Lewis and Clark's mission wasn't felt until the Western territories became states in the late 1800s. At that point, Americans began to realize how vast and even foreign the area of the Louisiana Purchase was. Throughout the decades of the late 1800s, wagon train after wagon train, and then railroads, brought hundreds of thousands of pioneers from Missouri to California and all points in between.

Without Lewis and Clark, those routes may never have been blazed for American settlers.

Lewis and Clark are truly two of the greatest heroes in American history, not just for leading their expedition from Missouri to the Pacific and back; how they led the expedition is what makes them true heroes.

Lewis and Clark used a combination of skill, fortitude, intelligence, and some luck to complete the greatest exploratory expedition in American history. Both men demonstrated incredible teamwork along the way, relying on each other's strengths to overcome some pretty incredible odds.

Achieving their ultimate goal of going to the Pacific and back was enough to make Lewis and Clark heroes, but perhaps just as important was that only one of the men in their expedition died during the journey.

That should tell anyone that, despite the incredible odds Lewis and Clark faced, they genuinely cared about the men in their party. For that alone, Lewis and Clark are true American heroes!

DID YOU KNOW?

- The expedition covered nearly 8,000 miles and split into two groups for a time on the return leg.

- Lewis cataloged 178 new plants and 122 animals. The pair also compiled more than 140 maps.

- Lewis was appointed governor of Upper Louisiana Territory (roughly the modern Upper Midwest) by President Jefferson in 1806. Although his life seemed to be on an upward trajectory after the expedition, he became an alcoholic and died in 1809 under mysterious circumstances. His death was first ruled a suicide, but some historians believe he was killed during a robbery.

- When the expedition arrived in what is now western Montana, they were greeted by creatures they had never seen before—grizzly bears! The bears proved to be somewhat troublesome as the expedition lost some supplies to them, but they suffered no casualties otherwise.

- Clark served as the governor of Missouri Territory from 1813 to 1820. As an example of how little Lewis and Clark were regarded during their lifetimes, Clark lost the election to be the first governor of the state of Missouri in 1820.

BABE RUTH
AMERICA'S FIRST SPORTS HERO

The term *"sports hero"* has become so common today that it is a bit of a cliché. There are plenty of phenomenal athletes in the United States, many of whom do some great things off the field, in addition to their sports careers. But there is little doubt that the modern American athlete is often put on a pedestal by the media and fans—many argue too much so— just for playing a game.

Yet it wasn't always this way.

Just under 100 years ago, when professional sports leagues were in their early years in the United States, there were no real big names. It was long before the Internet, or even television, for that matter, and advertisers were only beginning to see the value of placing ads in stadiums. Most professional athletes at that time, even the top ones, were for the most part anonymous.

But then came Babe Ruth. It wouldn't be an understatement to say that not only did Babe Ruth revolutionize baseball, he forever changed professional sports in America. With a larger than life persona, Babe Ruth captured the hearts and imaginations of Americans from coast to coast.

This was incredible given he played at a time when the vast majority only ever saw his picture in newspapers and *heard* him play on the radio. His bold personality and sometimes bad boy reputation just added to what were already the most impressive statistics ever compiled by a Major League player at the time.

He won numerous battle titles, was the first player to hit 500 home runs, and was the American League home-run champion 12 times. Perhaps the most incredible part of Ruth's playing career is that he was also a fairly good pitcher.

Ruth compiled a 94–46 record as a pitcher, a lifetime 2.28 ERA, and was the American League ERA leader in 1916. If you aren't familiar with baseball, it is almost unheard of for a good position player to be an even serviceable pitcher, or for a pitcher to be an even average hitter.

When compared to modern era baseball players, Ruth's career is even more astonishing. Ruth had no access to performance-enhancing drugs, didn't know what a personal trainer was, never saw a fitness/weight room, and didn't know the first thing about a proper diet. Babe loved to drink beer, eat hotdogs, and hit the ball out of the park!

After establishing himself as America's first sports hero, tragedy struck when Ruth was diagnosed with terminal cancer. But he faced the deadly disease bravely, allowing doctors to use experimental drugs and procedures on him that later became mainstream cancer treatments.

In life, Babe Ruth earned the love of the American people, and in death he gained their respect.

A TOUGH KID FROM A TOUGH TIME

Babe Ruth was born George Herman Ruth Junior on February 6, 1895 to first-generation German Americans in Baltimore, Maryland. Family life in the Ruth home was tough, to say the least. He was one of eight children born to George Senior and Katherine, but only one of two to survive infancy. Needless to say, medicine and medical facilities weren't as good back then. Life wasn't always easy within the Ruth family. George Junior struggled to hold down jobs for much of his life and when he finally settled in as a bar owner, he wasn't there to give George Junior much direction.

So, George Junior received his education about life on the hard-scrabble streets of Baltimore.

In the early 1900s, Baltimore was a gritty, industrial city with a large European immigrant population. George Junior spoke German at home with his family, but when he ran the streets, he learned English among other things. Repeated minor run-ins with the law resulted in George Junior being sent to a reformatory at age seven, where he would spend the next 12 years of his life.

Life in the reformatory was tough at times. George Junior was sometimes bullied by the older boys, the food was terrible, and he lived under strict rules administered by Catholic monks. Well, the last point was rather good for George Junior. The monks gave him the discipline he was lacking in his home and they also introduced him to baseball.

Once George Junior took the field, it was immediately clear to the monks and the other boys that he had a natural talent for the sport. He could hit *and* pitch, but it was his pitching ability that brought him to the attention of Jack Dunn, the owner of the Baltimore Orioles in 1914.

The Orioles were a minor league team at the time and a steppingstone for many Major League careers. Ruth signed with them when he was 19 as a highly touted prospect, quickly becoming known as Dunn's Babe.

But it didn't take Babe long to get called up to the Majors.

AN UNSTOPPABLE FORCE

Babe's meteoric rise through professional baseball began as soon as he suited up for his first game. To get his books in the black, Dunn sold his best players to Major League teams. Ruth was bought by the Boston Red Sox in July 1914, but it took him a while to earn a regular spot in the rotation.

It also took Babe some time to earn the respect of his fellow players and the fans.

After a brief stint in the Red Sox's minor league affiliate, Ruth returned to the Red Sox as a pitcher *and* position player in 1915. Things began to improve for Ruth and the Sox at that point, as he recorded good stats that year and the Red Sox won the World Series.

Since he was a lefty, Ruth's skills as a pitcher were in high demand, but he was never satisfied and wanted to play every day. After many Major League players went to fight in World War I during the 1918 season, Ruth got his chance to play first base and other positions regularly.

He began lighting up the scoreboard and the imagination of fans, but almost as quickly as it started, he was sold to the

New York Yankees in 1920 for the sum of $100,000—incredible at the time. This is when the legend of Babe Ruth began.

The Boston Red Sox would not win another World Series until 2004, with their hardcore fans believing they were cursed for selling Ruth. For Ruth, the big lights and extensive press of the Big Apple allowed him to develop the image of America's first sports hero.

A TRUE ICON

As Babe Ruth set and broke batting record after batting record with the New York Yankees, the press caught wind of the sometimes lurid details of his lifestyle. Although married, Ruth was seen about town with many different women on his arm.

After his first wife, Helen, died in a fire in 1929, he married his second wife, Claire, later that year. But Babe's second marriage didn't slow him down either.

The cornerstone of Babe's lifestyle was his love of beer. He would have the bathtubs of his hotel rooms filled with iced beer so he could have a few drinks after hitting the bars and nightclubs until the early morning hours. Teammates were amazed at how much Babe could drink and seemingly remain sober; he was known to have some of his best games after nights of heavy drinking.

A moral clause that he signed with the Yankees in 1922 was supposedly meant to slow down the playboy but did little good. America was a much more socially conservative country in 1922, and the owners of the Yankees were worried that Ruth's reputation would become public and hurt the image of the team. Well, Babe's antics did become public, but they only seemed to endear him more to America.

Like everyone, although he was rich and famous, Babe Ruth was a flawed individual with whom people could identify. There was also a bit of the *"lifestyles of the rich and famous"* effect taking place. People read and listened to whatever report they could find about Ruth, secretly wishing that they could have his life.

Babe Ruth was perhaps the first major American celebrity through which people lived vicariously.

Ruth's hero status continued to grow as his career progressed and became legendary after he retired in 1935. He became the most prized baseball card in the early years of sports trading cards and kids across America tried to replicate the Big Bambino's signature stance and swing when they played little league.

But Babe's final battle was no game.

In 1946, doctors found a cancerous growth at the base of Babe Ruth's skull. Fighting the disease with all his energy like the hero that he was, Babe underwent many new procedures, including chemotherapy. Although the cancer briefly went into remission, Babe Ruth succumbed to the fatal disease on August 16, 1948 at the age of 53.

Number 3 may have been gone, but he was far from forgotten. Babe Ruth's legend grew after his death until he became the most recognized American athlete of all time. Babe's on the field success brought Americans together during World War I, the Spanish flu pandemic of 1918, and the early years of the

Great Depression. He was truly a man of the people, with whom anyone could relate and he, in turn, could relate to the average American.

There have been many great sports heroes since Babe Ruth, but they all owe a debt of gratitude to the Big Bambino — America's first true sports hero.

DID YOU KNOW?

- In 1921, Ruth had a daughter, Dorothy, with one of his mistresses. His first wife adopted Dorothy as her daughter. Ruth later adopted his second wife's daughter, Julia.

- As a sign of his hero status, after retiring, Ruth played in some *"old-timers"* exhibition games that drew large crowds.

- Babe was one of the first professional athletes to entertain the troops. In the early years of World War II, Babe visited and played in exhibition games for American troops.

- Ruth attempted to land a managerial job with a Major League team for years but was essentially blacklisted due to his playboy image.

- He was one of five players selected in the first year of the Baseball Hall of Fame in 1936. He was selected less than one year after retiring from his final team, the Boston Braves.

BENJAMIN FRANKLIN
AN AMERICAN RENAISSANCE MAN

You've probably heard the term *"Renaissance man"* at some point in your life. If you haven't, or if you have and aren't quite sure what it means, it simply refers to a person who is knowledgeable and proficient in many areas. The term originally referred to Renaissance artists such as Leonardo da Vinci and Michelangelo, who were skilled artists, scientists, and scholars.

The term may be overused a bit today, but there are still plenty of Renaissance men and women in the world. But no American Renaissance man was as important or impactful as Benjamin Franklin.

Benjamin Franklin is best known in the United States for being one of the founding fathers and one of only a few non-presidents to appear on U.S. currency.

But Benjamin Franklin was so much more. He was a man who never rested, tirelessly

conducting countless scientific experiments, inventing many things we use every day. Franklin also helped organize the United States Post Office and used his immense store of knowledge and language skills to further the American agenda overseas as a diplomat.

Truly, Benjamin Franklin was America's first Renaissance Man, as he brought the light of knowledge and civilization to a wild, new country that desperately needed it. Franklin may not have led armies or served as president, but his numerous contributions to early American society can't be placed in any single category, and for that he is one of this country's greatest heroes.

A MAN OF THE ENLIGHTENMENT

Benjamin Franklin was born on January 17, 1706 to a rather average colonial family. Among his family were Puritans who resisted the British crown and indentured servants who were little better off than slaves. Benjamin came from quite a large family. He was one of 17 children whom his father, Josiah, sired with two different wives. Benjamin was born at the tail end of the family; he was the eighth child of his mother, Abiah's, ten children.

Despite being one of the brightest men of his time — and quite possibly in all of American history — young Benjamin had little formal education. Since his family was so large, it was nearly impossible for his father to send him to an expensive private school. Benjamin did attend a private school for a couple of years, but when his father was no longer able to pay for the tuition, he was forced to withdraw.

But that was quite alright for Franklin. He was always a free spirit and often felt constrained by buildings and institutions. He taught himself the classics and began learning French and other modern European languages at a young age. He also read about some of the great philosophers of the European

Enlightenment, such as John Locke, Gottfried Leibniz, and Nicolas de Condorcet. It was in the writings of those and other philosophers where young Franklin found inspiration to question authority, challenge himself, and try to make society better.

Benjamin applied his new-found ideas on his first job—working for his older brother's newspaper, *The New-England Courant*. The paper wasn't much different than the hundreds of other papers that were popping up daily all over the Thirteen Colonies and then disappearing just as quickly. It reported a lot of local gossip and other trivial matters, but after the brothers began getting more political, James was jailed in 1722. Young Benjamin ran the paper for a couple of weeks but then left without his brother's permission.

Benjamin was 17 and ready to see the world. He knew that, although Boston was his home, his opportunities there were limited. If he wanted to see the world and live in a truly happening place, he needed to head south to Philadelphia.

Franklin quickly found his place in Philadelphia. He had no problem finding work among the city's numerous newspapers and after a while began printing newspapers of his own. Franklin even published the first German-language newspaper in America!

Benjamin also made numerous connections among the Philadelphia literati, which is where he got his first taste of organizing. Franklin gathered influential Philadelphia citizens to help found one of the oldest libraries in America in 1731. At this point, Franklin realized that politics is an art that requires plenty of patience and an ability to be diplomatic. He never came across strong but nearly always got what he wanted.

A SCIENTIST ALWAYS AT WORK

Franklin was a man who never rested. When he wasn't running a newspaper, he was in his lab conducting experiments or inventing new things. As he once wrote, *"Well done is better than well said."* Franklin always had to be doing something.

Franklin is best known for his experiments on electricity. You've no doubt seen a representation of him flying a kite that gets hit by lightning, right? He may or may not have been one of the first to conduct such an experiment (it is today probably more legend than anything), but he did successfully apply the idea that lightning can be ground when he invented the lightning rod.

He also invented bifocal glasses, a special stove, and the glass harmonica, among a plethora of other devices.

Franklin also had a deep interest in the weather, geography, geology, and cartography.

So how did Franklin share all of this with the world in the era before the Internet and television? He simply used his publishing skills and background to produce an annual almanac known as *Poor Richard's Almanack*. Published from 1732 to 1758 under a pen name, the almanac shared Franklin's knowledge of his inventions with America, offered predictions on weather patterns useful for farmers, and gave fairly accurate population statistics. Franklin also used the publication to showcase his philosophical skills.

Franklin's aphorisms have become so common in America that you've probably used a few of them and aren't even aware of their origins: *"Haste makes waste," "When you're good to others, you're best to yourself," "Lost time is never found again,"* and perhaps the most repeated, *"A penny saved is a penny earned."*

By the time Benjamin became America's first Postmaster General in 1775, he was an old man. But his vigorous nature kept him going so that, when the American Revolution occurred, he became an integral part of it. Due to his vast network of connections in America and Europe—and also because of the great respect he earned over his lifetime of accomplishments—Washington, Jefferson, and the other Founding Fathers sought his support.

Jefferson was the primary architect of the Declaration of Independence, Madison was the brain behind the Constitution, and Washington won America's freedom on the battlefield; so, what then was Franklin's role in American Independence?

Well, Franklin was the American ambassador to France from 1776 to 1785. It may sound like it was a fun post for the then elderly Franklin, but his work in France proved to be decisive in the American Revolution. It is important to remember that America was not yet a true country: its money was worthless, and the Continental Army was often underequipped. Besides the material problems the Patriots faced, they also needed their cause to be accepted by other countries. This is what Franklin was doing in France.

Through a combination of Franklin's diplomatic efforts and a couple of key battlefield victories by Washington, the Americans finally got the alliance they needed from the French, which ultimately pushed their cause to victory.

Without Benjamin Franklin and the French alliance, America may not have become an independent nation!

A MULTI-FACETED HERO

Benjamin Franklin is one of the most easily recognizable heroes in our book. Nearly every American knows his name, and most would recognize his image. This is, of course, for good reason: Franklin had an extremely profound effect on our country. His scientific endeavors helped propel America from being a backwoods appendage of Europe into a strong, industrious, and independent nation.

Franklin's leadership was also indispensable. As the Patriot leaders were searching for allies around the world, and anyone who could bring potential allies to their cause, Benjamin Franklin stepped up and brought the French to America, which helped Washington achieve victory.

A true Renaissance man, Benjamin Franklin was always hard at work looking for ways to constructively apply his skills and knowledge, while at the same time learning new things, whether it be a scientific theory, foreign language, or important historical events. Always practical, Franklin believed that everything he learned should apply to the real world, which he demonstrated time and time again until he died in 1790 at the age of 84.

All of these factors make Benjamin Franklin one of the first and foremost of American heroes.

DID YOU KNOW?

- Another term for a Renaissance Man is a *polymath*.

- Franklin earned the nickname The First American before and during the early stages of the American Revolution. He made trips to England before the war to argue for peace. After the war began, he was the ambassador to France. For these reasons, Benjamin Franklin was the most recognized American in Europe.

- Franklin was never officially married. His common-law wife Deborah Read (1708–1774) was married, but her husband deserted her in 1727. Under the marriage laws at the time, Read was unable to get a divorce based on desertion.

- Franklin had one daughter and two sons. His oldest son, William (1730–1813), was illegitimate, although Franklin gave him his name and raised him. William sided with the Crown during the Revolution, which permanently destroyed his relationship with Benjamin.

- Although Franklin lived to old age, especially for the period, he suffered from problems related to being overweight for most of his life. He died from inflammation of the lungs, which was likely aggravated by his obesity.

SITTING BULL
A NOBLE WARRIOR UNTIL THE END

As we discussed in an earlier chapter, Lewis and Clark's expedition through the newly acquired Louisiana Territory had profound and long-term effects on the history of the United States. The journey brought the vast territory under the control of the United States, but it would still be several decades before there was any large-scale settlement in the region.

The California gold rush of the 1840s brought tens of thousands of settlers through the West, but most simply passed through the Great Plains and the Rocky Mountains on their way to California. However, just before the Civil War, things began to drastically change.

The Colorado gold rush of 1858 attracted thousands to that region and another gold rush in the Dakota Territory in the 1870s brought thousands more to what is today western South Dakota.

These gold rushes, and the later settlement and development of the Great Plains and the Rocky Mountains, took pioneers into direct conflict with many Native American tribes, most notably the three major tribes of the Sioux nation.

The Sioux were divided into three primary tribes—Lakota, Nakota, and Dakota—that called the upper Great Plains their home. They were a semi-nomadic people who survived by hunting bison and raiding their weaker neighbors. Lewis and Clark noted that the Sioux were a proud people who would rather go to war than lose face.

When American settlement finally began to encroach on Sioux lands in the middle of the 1800s, it led to bloodshed and war. The first major war between the U.S. and the Sioux was the Dakota War of 1862. In that war, the Americans vanquished most of the Dakota Sioux from the state of Minnesota.

But even more costly battles and wars would follow.

The Sioux found themselves in a nearly impossible situation by the late 1800s. They knew that they couldn't hope to defeat the superior numbers and technology of the American military, yet they kept fighting. Some Sioux leaders, such as Crazy Horse, offered no real plans or goals other than to kill as many Whites as possible. But among the chaos and violence of the time, a Sioux leader came forward who offered a different course of action.

Chief Sitting Bull was viewed by his people as a spiritual man capable of great visions. He was respected by the White military and civilians alike as a reasonable, fair, and wise leader. Sitting Bull never quit fighting for his people, but he was wise enough to know when the war was over, and blood was being shed for no reason.

He eventually endeared himself to Americans when he toured in Buffalo Bill Cody's Wild West Show for a few years, presenting an image of a noble, wise American Indian.

Because of his efforts on behalf of his people, and the way he went about it, Sitting Bull is recognized as a true hero by Americans of all backgrounds.

A WARRIOR FROM BIRTH

Sitting Bull was born as Jumping Badger, probably in 1831, somewhere in Dakota Territory to a Lakota chief named Jumping Bull. He was named after his father when he completed a successful raid on some Crow Indians when he was a teenager.

Young Jumping Badger/Sitting Bull was already known among his people as a bright, introspective young man, but the raid on the Crows gave him the respect he would later need to lead the Lakota.

Sitting Bull was well known for his bravery, but he was also known for being slow, which in the Sioux languages meant he was thoughtful. The young warrior led many warbands against other American Indians, White settlers, and the U.S. Army, yet he was always cautious, never wanting to risk the lives of his warriors unnecessarily.

His first known combat against the U.S. military came during the Dakota-U.S. War of 1862. Although that war was fought primarily in Minnesota, the military attacked some Sioux camps in the Dakotas, including one where Sitting Bull lived, in July 1864. The limited action gave Sitting Bull his first taste of the power of the American military; he knew that it was a force that could wipe his people out, but he also knew that he had to stand against it.

When Sitting Bull wasn't leading warbands, he was

interpreting the dreams and visions of his people. He was also known to have many visions of his own, which his people believe came true. In one particularly important vision, Sitting Bull claims he saw soldiers falling like grasshoppers into the Lakota camp. Many of his people at first thought that this was an ill or evil omen, but he assured them that it meant they would have a great victory.

He had the vision in 1876, just before the Battle of Little Bighorn. We'll get to that in a minute.

As Sitting Bull's reputation as a leader, warrior, and mystic increased among the Sioux, he became the chief of the Hunkpapa band of Lakota. With the promotion came great responsibility—not only would he have to watch over his people, he would also have to confer with other Sioux chiefs on matters of peace and war.

Sitting Bull's first major diplomatic and military test came when he aligned with Oglala Lakota Chief Red Cloud in Red Cloud's War (1866–1868). The war was fought for control of the Powder River Country in what is today Wyoming and Montana. The ever-encroaching Americans wanted the region for ranching, settlement, and possibly gold mining, but the Sioux were not so keen to give it up.

And Sitting Bull didn't want to end the war, even after Red Cloud agreed to end hostilities. Sitting Bull continued to attack U.S. outposts in a series of lightning hit-and-run raids before he retreated to Dakota Territory to come up with a new strategy.

The Treaty of Fort Laramie in 1868 created the Great Sioux Reservation, which was essentially the western half of South

Dakota. The discovery of gold in the Black Hills in 1874 created a rush of American settlers to the region.

It also set Sitting Bull on a crash course with the U.S. Army.

THE BATTLE THAT MADE HIM A HERO

President Ulysses Grant wanted to open the West and get its gold at any cost. Remember, Grant was a Union general in the Civil War, so he was used to knocking a few heads if he didn't get things his way.

He first sent the infamous Lieutenant Colonel George Armstrong Custer to the Dakota Territory with the cavalry as a show of force. Custer may have made some of the settlers in the Black Hills feel good, but his arrival only seemed to make Sitting Bull more resolved to resist.

When President Grant ordered all Sioux to move to the Great Sioux Reservation in late 1875, it was essentially a declaration of war. Sitting Bull met with other Sioux and Cheyenne leaders to develop a plan of resistance. They decided that they would give Custer and the 7th Cavalry Regiment blood!

Throughout the winter and spring of 1876, more and more displaced Sioux and Cheyenne made their way to Sitting Bull's traveling camp on the plains. By the summer of 1876, it was thousands strong and the leaders of other tribes and bands, such as Crazy Horse, deferred to Sitting Bull's leadership. Most importantly, the number of warriors swelled to more than 2,000.

The United States Army was embarking on a major campaign to rid the upper Great Plains of what they saw as recalcitrant

Native American tribes, when Custer and the 7th Cavalry came upon Sitting Bull's camp near a place called Little Bighorn, in what is today Montana.

The headstrong Custer didn't want to wait for reinforcements, so he marched his men right into Sitting Bull's trap and the U.S. Army's greatest battlefield loss to an American Indian foe. The total death count for the Army was 268 men, including Custer, but the American Indian allies had little time to celebrate their victory.

The full weight of the U.S. Army came down on Sitting Bull, forcing him to go on the run.

A NEW KIND OF HERO

Sitting Bull and many of his people fled north to Canada, where they were given temporary asylum. Unable to live off the land as they had done on the American plains, and also homesick, Sitting Bull returned to the United States and surrendered to the Army on July 19, 1881.

The proud Lakota chief was declared a prisoner of war and spent two years in prison, but it was then that his hero status began to grow, with Whites as well as American Indians.

To American Indians, Sitting Bull was seen as a heroic defender of their way of life, who was as clever and wise as he was brave. To White Americans, Sitting Bull was viewed as representative of what they respected about American Indians. He was noble and brave, yet willing to accept the inevitable victory of American culture.

Sitting Bull was so willing to become part of American culture that he joined Buffalo Bill Cody's *Buffalo Bill's Wild West* show in late 1884 and 1885. He toured the United States and Canada with Buffalo Bill, Annie Oakley, and other notable American Indian leaders. Many of the only known photographs of Sitting Bull were taken while he was touring with the show.

The former chief earned a nice chunk of money, which allowed him to retire to the Standing Rock Reservation in Dakota Territory in comfort.

Or so he thought.

Sitting Bull mostly retired from tribal politics, but when the American Indian spiritual and political movement known as the Ghost Dance came to Standing Rock, he allowed it to flourish. The government set out to shut the Ghost Dance movement down wherever possible.

On December 15, 1890, federal officers attempted to arrest Sitting Bull for planning to leave the reservation and for taking part in the Ghost Dance movement. A struggle ensued with Sitting Bull, several of his supporters, and some federal officers dying in a shootout.

A COMPLEX HERO

Sitting Bull is one of the most complex heroes in our book. He wore many different hats in his lifetime, including warrior, leader, diplomat, and entertainer. He brought hope to his people, smiles to the faces of Americans, and was a bridge of peace and reconciliation between Americans and American Indians.

The tragic end to Sitting Bull's life ensured that he'd be remembered as a man who stood by his principles, even in old age, until his death.

DID YOU KNOW?

- Sitting Bull had at least five wives during his life, some concurrently, as was allowed under Lakota traditions. He sired at least three children and adopted others. Needless to say, Sitting Bull's tepee was quite big!

- Today, the Standing Rock Indian Reservation is located in both South Dakota and North Dakota. Although most of the reservation is in north-central South Dakota, part of it is in south-central North Dakota.

- Sitting Bull's remains are believed to be interred near Mobridge, South Dakota, although the claim has been disputed.

- The United States Army's campaign against Sitting Bull in 1876 is commonly known as the Great Sioux War.

- Although Sitting Bull was the foremost leader of the Plains Indians in the late 1800s, not all tribes of the region joined him. The Crow had seen their lands reduced due to the more numerous and stronger Sioux tribes, so they joined the U.S. Army against Sitting Bull.

MOLLY PITCHER
THE FIRST AMERICAN WAR HEROINE

Throughout world history, women have rallied to the war effort of their countries along with the men. Women have primarily served in support roles, but those positions have been just as important. During World War II, women kept the factories running that produced the weapons, and in earlier wars, it was women who nursed the wounded back to health.

Sometimes, though, women had to get directly involved in the fight.

Our next American hero is a woman who has attained legendary status—Molly Pitcher. You see, Molly Pitcher was the first American war heroine, but her true identity is shrouded in mystery. The story goes that she was by her husband's side at the Battle of Monmouth in the American Revolution, bringing water to him and his comrades in a pitcher, thus the nickname.

After he was wounded, she took his place. There have been different versions of the story and multiple women have been identified as the true Molly Pitcher, which only serves to demonstrate the importance of her story.

Molly Pitcher was the epitome of the early American spirit—

free, independent, and strong — embodied in the story of one woman.

MARY LUDWIG HAYS

The most probable Molly Pitcher was Mary Ludwig Hays. Mary was born near Trenton, New Jersey but later moved to Pennsylvania where she met and married William Hays (also known as John Hays). When the American Revolution broke out, William volunteered for the struggling Continental Army and Mary joined as a camp follower, cooking, cleaning, and doing other domestic duties when needed.

The first couple of years were tough for the Continental Army, which included them losing the American capital of Philadelphia to the British. But their big break came when the British surrendered Philadelphia and began the long march back to New York City in June 1778.

The Continental Army followed and caught up with them at Monmouth on June 28, which is when the legend of Molly Pitcher was born.

The Battle of Monmouth was incredibly important to the Continental Army, which had lost numerous engagements in a row to the British. After the French announced they were joining the war on the side of the Americans, the British retreated from Philadelphia back to the safety of New York. George Washington caught up to them and a pitched battle ensued.

It was a hot, humid afternoon. The Continentals took everything the British threw at them and gave it right back. William Hays and his men kept firing their muskets and cannons at the British to the point of exhaustion, but there was Mary with pitchers of water to replenish the men and cool the cannons. When William was overcome by the heat and passed out, Mary took his spot at the cannon and kept firing at the British.

After the war, Mary and William returned to Pennsylvania and after William died Mary married a man named John McCauley.

Although the state of Pennsylvania recognized Mary for her wartime service, she wasn't known as Molly Pitcher until she died in 1832. The legend of Molly Pitcher was born when American Revolution veteran Joseph Plum Martin published his memoirs in 1830. It took a few years for the legend to circulate, though.

Information moved slowly back then, and Martin's memoirs weren't the most riveting read of the period; but, by the mid-1800s, the story of Molly Pitcher began to be known around America.

OTHER MOLLY PITCHERS?

Although Mary Ludwig Hays is the most likely woman to be the true Molly Pitcher, there have been other women who have made the claim. Another woman from Pennsylvania, named Margaret Corbin, was known to have followed her husband John into battle against the Hessians in New York. John was killed and Margaret was later recognized by the Continental Army for her service, which was said to include manning a cannon after her husband was killed.

Another potential candidate was a woman named Deborah

Sampson, who disguised herself as a man and served in the Continental Army. Sampson and Corbin were the only two women in the American Revolution to be given veteran's benefits, although Mary Hays was given some benefits by the state of Pennsylvania.

A BRAVE AMERICAN WOMAN

There is a strong likelihood that the legend of Molly Pitcher was based on more than one woman—or all of the three women. Mary Hays was probably the original Molly Pitcher, but as knowledge of the others began circulating in the 1800s, details of their lives were added to the legend.

Eventually, much like many of the other heroes in our book, Molly Pitcher became a sort of idealized archetype of a woman in early America. Like Molly Pitcher, women from that era were expected to take care of traditional domestic duties, such as cleaning and cooking, but the ravages of war gave them even more responsibilities.

Women in the American Revolutionary War era, especially the camp followers like Molly Pitcher, had to make sure that the men were strong enough and equipped to fight. If need be, they also had to step in and do some fighting themselves.

Molly Pitcher demonstrated that American women weren't afraid to fight for their families and nation, and for that reason, she is America's first war heroine.

DID YOU KNOW?

- William Hays worked as a barber before the war.

- A World War II cargo ship was named the SS *Molly Pitcher*. It was torpedoed by a German U-boat and lost in 1943.

- According to one account, an enemy cannonball fired straight at her *"carrying away all the lower part of her petticoat,"* although she was otherwise unscathed.

- Mary Hays was buried in her adopted hometown of Carlisle, Pennsylvania. A monument that states she is the one and only Molly Pitcher marks her grave. The monument includes a statue of her standing over a cannon.

- Reports of Mary Hays depict her as a tough woman who wasn't afraid to use colorful language, which lines up well with a woman who served at the front in wartime.

JESSE JAMES
THE ORIGINAL AMERICAN ANTI-HERO

We've already met a couple of American heroes who somewhat stretch the definition of the phrase—Robert E. Lee and Sitting Bull. Both of those men engaged in active military campaigns against the United States that led to many deaths.

For that reason alone, they were hated by large segments of the American population, yet they were also fighting legitimate wars and represented the ideas of thousands, or even millions, of people. General Lee and Sitting Bull also fought for causes. Although they may have been lost causes, by all accounts, both men believed in what they were doing and were willing to go to the grave over their beliefs.

So, General Lee and Sitting Bull can be classified as true rebels, yet still legitimate heroes. On the other hand, Jesse James was an anti-hero, and the first notable American to be classified as such.

An anti-hero is a person who may have many of the qualities of a hero but is usually an antagonist instead of a protagonist. An anti-hero can be brave and is usually charismatic, yet he or she is almost always opposed to the system and society's norms. Still, anti-heroes are sometimes viewed sympathetically, especially in the United States.

When Jesse James and his band of outlaws robbed banks and trains across the Midwestern United States in the mid to late-1800s, they stoked the imagination of millions of Americans. Although everyone knew what the handsome outlaw was doing was wrong, many secretly wanted him to get away with his crimes. After all, as many thought, he was just *"sticking it to"* the banks and the trains, which were often viewed negatively at the time.

So, Jesse James became the first great American anti-hero. After he died, his legend only continued to grow and the secret admiration for him turned to reverence among many. He became the hero in fictional accounts, people chose his name for their newborn sons, and legions of Americans claim ancestry from the Missouri outlaw.

Jesse James continues to be one of the most popular figures in America despite his violent and sordid background.

YOUNG JESSE JAMES

Jesse Woodson James was born on September 5, 1847 in rural Clay County, Missouri. It was certainly a quite different place—and one could argue, a vastly different world—to northwestern Missouri today, or even the United States, for that matter. Missouri was one of the newer states in 1847 but was quickly being settled by people from all regions of the U.S.

The region of Missouri where the James family lived was known as *"Little Dixie"* because many of the settlers were from Kentucky and Tennessee. The settlers in Little Dixie owned slaves and also identified with the South in the growing sectional tension that was taking place in America before the war.

Young Jesse worked on the family farm with his brother Frank, his stepfather, and the family's slaves, but by the late 1850s, it was clear that Jesse's formative years would be marked by violence.

After the Kansas-Nebraska Act of 1854 left the question of slavery up to the popular vote of the citizens of Kansas Territory, violence almost immediately broke out between *"free soil"* and anti-slavery advocates against pro-slavery groups. The violence that became known as Bleeding Kansas was heavily influenced by pro-slavery militants from Missouri, which included Jesse James' neighbors and family.

There is no evidence that young Jesse was involved in the Bleeding Kansas violence, but once the Civil War began in 1861, Frank James joined local pro-Confederate partisans.

Jesse heard the stories his brother Frank told of attacking pro-Union militias and settlers in Missouri, sometimes their innocent neighbors. By the time Jesse was 15, he was ready to join his brother in the fight.

Frank rode with the infamous William Quantrill and his band of pro-Confederate partisan guerrillas, who raided Union forces and towns in Kentucky, Missouri, and Kansas. It's important to remember that Jesse was doing all this at a time in his life when most kids his age today are playing video games or talking on the phone with their buddies and crushes. It is unknown how many men Jesse killed at this young age, but it was certainly a fair number.

The fighting in the border states was also a different type of warfare. Jesse and Frank learned how to rob the enemy of its gold, sabotage supply lines, destroy telegraph lines, and — more than occasionally — kill civilians.

When the war ended, Jesse was only 18, but he had seen and experienced more than most will in a lifetime. He had been beaten half to death, shot, and had killed several people. With his family destitute because of the war, and no job prospects to speak of, Jesse decided to turn his skills in riding, shooting, and robbing to use.

THE WAR NEVER ENDED

Jesse and Frank James were unrepentant Confederates, which is largely part of how the legend began. There is no doubt that Jesse committed his crimes for himself, but when the press learned of his Confederate background, it made for a good story. He became a romantic anti-hero who was fighting against the system, an unrepentant Confederate, and a rebel with a true cause.

Jesse's good looks certainly helped his image, and he was said to even be a bit chivalrous at times. All of this led to sensationalized news reports of his exploits, which only seemed to feed his growing notoriety.

Truly, Jesse James was not only America's first anti-hero, he was America's first celebrity criminal.

It all began not long after the Civil War ended, although for Jesse, the war never really ended. He and Frank started looking up many of their old comrades from Quantrill's crew and, before too long, they committed the first daylight bank robberies in American history.

From bank robberies, the brothers progressed to the even more daring crime of train robbery in 1873. Jesse's reputation grew when he brought in more members to his gang, such as the Younger brothers.

But Jesse's success brought unwanted attention and enemies.

The state governments only had limited success in trying to track down Jesse James, and there was no FBI yet, so Jesse and his band of robbers only had to keep moving across state lines to avoid capture.

While they were in Missouri, they often hid in plain sight, harbored by former Confederate soldiers and partisans. Still, there were rewards out for Jesse's capture — dead or alive — in several Midwestern states, and the Pinkerton Detective Agency was paid hefty sums by the railroad companies to stop him.

Despite all the heat on Jesse James, though, it was a bit of a freak incident that ended up being his downfall.

PRIDE COMES BEFORE THE FALL

By late 1876, Jesse James and his boys were believing their hype. Many reports painted them as a modern-day Robin Hood and his merry band, although Jesse wasn't known to spread the wealth from his heists around much. Jesse thought that he was untouchable so, in September, he and his gang rode up to Northfield, Minnesota to rob what they believed was a bank owned by a wealthy Republican.

At the time, the Republicans were the advocates of Reconstruction in the South, which included disenfranchising former Confederates and enfranchising former slaves. Jesse and Frank heard that the Northfield bank was owned by Republican interests. They were partially correct—Benjamin Butler, a Union general in the Civil War and commander of New Orleans during Reconstruction, was a shareholder in the bank.

So, Jesse James decided that robbing the Northfield, Minnesota bank would be a good way to strike out against the system and add to his growing purse at the same time.

Jesse also wanted to add to his reputation; to do that, he had to pull off a brazen robbery for a lot of loot.

On September 7, 1876, Jesse James and several members of their gang rode into Northfield and took over the First National Bank.

Things immediately went wrong.

Bank employees resisted and the gang members responded by beating, shooting, and killing an employee. But if Jesse and his boys thought they were just going to waltz in and do whatever they wanted in Northfield, they were sorely mistaken.

Minnesota was a long way from Missouri—too far for comfort. Jesse and his boys didn't have any contacts up there and the mystique of his legend also didn't seem to have permeated the icy soil of the state. To make matters worse for Jesse, there was a gun club meeting in Northfield that day and it was the beginning of the hunting season in Minnesota.

Jesse James was lucky to get out of Minnesota alive!

After losing most of his gang, Jesse made it back to Missouri where he lived in semi-retirement until he was murdered by Bob Ford, one of his former gang members, on April 3, 1882.

Or *did* Ford kill him? Rumors abounded of Jesse James' survival, supposedly as part of a ploy by Ford to help him escape justice.

A TRUE AMERICAN OUTLAW

The mysterious circumstances surrounding the death of Jesse James only helped to add to the already larger-than-life legend that he was. By the time he died, he was a hero to many Americans. Former Confederates saw him as a hero who never gave up and a growing class of criminals viewed him as someone to emulate.

His brazen daylight bank robberies and train robberies were copied by later notable old west outlaws such as the Dalton Boys and Butch Cassidy and the Sundance Kid.

Most importantly, though, is the fact that Jesse James continues to inspire Americans more than 100 years after his death. Yes, Jesse James was a criminal and even a cold-blooded killer, but he invokes the rebel spirit in all of us.

Jesse James, the great American anti-hero, will no doubt continue to be the subject of films and television shows for some time to come. There is no doubt that America loves its bad boys!

DID YOU KNOW?

- One of the Confederate guerilla leaders Jesse James served under during the Civil War was William *"Bloody Bill"* Anderson. Anderson was responsible for leading several ambushes of Union soldiers in Missouri and attacks on pro-Union civilians.

- Jesse married his first cousin, Zerelda Mimms, in 1874. The couple had four children, although only two survived into adulthood.

- Not long after his death, Jesse James became the subject of several pulp fiction novels. He has been portrayed in dozens of films and television shows since the 1920s, often sympathetically.

- Jesse's son, Jesse E. James, was charged but acquitted of an 1898 train robbery. He later became a lawyer and wrote a book about his father's life, *Jesse James, My Father*.

- As a testament to his hero status, there are three museums dedicated to Jesse James in Missouri.

ALEXANDER GRAHAM BELL
CONNECTING AMERICA

For most of us, it is nearly impossible to envision life without our cellphones. Let's face it, cellphones have become like appendages of our arms; we can't go anywhere without them and we're always checking our messages or our friends' status updates.

No doubt part of the modern obsession with cellphones is based on vanity—checking to see how many likes our latest social media posts have—but it is also due to the reality of our modern world. Cellphones are now compact computers; not just for checking work emails but also for doing work right on the phone.

Cellphones have evolved from being merely mobile phones into something much more important. But the cellphone wouldn't be possible without the invention of the landline phone first, which was thanks to American inventor Alexander Graham Bell.

Although not born in the United States, Bell was a true American hero who gave one of the greatest gifts to this country, and the world, when he invented the telephone. The invention of the telephone was one of the final steps to bridge the vastness that was the American continent at the time: the railroads allowed people to physically travel across America and, in 1876, Bell's patent for the first telephone made speaking to people instantly, coast to coast, a reality.

Bell would later invent other important devices, do some early work with deaf people, and—like Thomas Edison—was a keen entrepreneur who knew how to market his inventions. But Bell is best known for the invention of the telephone, which provided the basis for countless later inventions.

A NURTURING OF INQUIRY

You've probably noticed that many of America's greatest heroes and heroines had tough early lives. These great men and women often had to overcome incredible challenges and they endured great struggles, which ultimately helped to make them the heroes and heroines they later became. Alexander Graham Bell, though, had a much different path to becoming a hero.

Alexander was born on March 3, 1847, in Edinburgh, Scotland to Alexander Melville Bell and Eliza Bell. Alexander Melville was a professor of speech at the University of Edinburgh when Alexander was born.

You're probably familiar with the nurture versus nature argument, which questions whether a person's destiny is determined by their upbringing or genetics. Well, in Alexander Graham Bell's case, he was the recipient of both.

He was no doubt imbued with an incredible amount of natural intelligence and genius but, unlike Thomas Edison, for example, Bell's father nurtured his natural talents.

Young Alexander was given free rein by his parents to study what he wanted. In the process, he developed some useful inventions, such as a wheat de-husking machine that was used at a local flour mill.

But the event that had the biggest impact on Alexander Graham Bell came at the age of 12. His mother had been suffering from deteriorating hearing for several years and she finally became deaf. At that point, Alexander made a vow that he would dedicate his life to making people hear better and bringing people closer.

Alexander enrolled at Edinburgh University and later the University College London, but it was soon clear that he was well advanced of his fellow students. Bell was a polyglot and delved into all the fields required to work with deaf people from around the world.

Despite the early successes in his life and his incredible potential, Alexander seemed content. He was happy to teach the deaf and help his father with publications. He knew he was doing important, hands-on work, but when his brother Melville died in 1870, things changed.

The Bell family moved to Canada and, almost overnight, Alexander became much more ambitious. It wasn't that Alexander had no drive—far from it—but in England he seemed to have exhausted his challenges.

Challenges need to be overcome for one to become a hero.

"MR. WATSON, COME HERE, I WANT TO SEE YOU"

Bell lived in Canada for about a year, and in 1871 he moved to the United States, where his creative and entrepreneurial skills flourished. Bell made good money teaching deaf children how to speak, through his father's System of Visible Speech.

However, he didn't rest on his laurels; his desire to explore the limits of human knowledge and to make a monumental difference in the world was just too great.

With the help of a wealthy benefactor, Alexander was able to work on his projects fulltime in Boston by 1872. Working long hours with little sleep or food, Alexander toiled on his telephone project with his trusty assistant, Thomas Watson, who was quite an accomplished engineer in his own right.

The idea of the telephone was based on the technology of the telegraph, which sent messages via electrical lines over long distances. The reality is that, although Bell ultimately won the first patent for the telephone, several other men had invented their own devices.

The best devices used electromagnetic transmitters and receivers that were capable of reading voices. Inventor Elisha Gray and Alexander Graham Bell both filed patents for their phones in 1876, with Gray submitting his in February.

Bell filed his patent on March 7, 1876, even before his device was successfully used. Three days later, though, Bell proved the worth of his invention when he said to Watson—who was out of earshot in the next room— *"Mr. Watson, come here, I want to see you."* The telephone worked!

The rest, as they would say, is history.

THE ORIGINAL WORLD WIDE WEB

Bell stayed busy after inventing his phone by focusing his energies on business and science. He invented several other devices, such as a metal detector and an early air conditioning system, but he dedicated most of his life to connecting the world by the telephone. Bell knew that it would take money and ambition to make his dream come true, so with the help of his father-in-law, he established the Bell Telephone Company in 1877.

The Bell Telephone Company was remarkably successful, spawning subsidiaries such as the American Telephone and Telegraph Company in 1885, which later became AT&T.

By the early 1900s, telephone lines were strewn across the vast United States, reaching areas where there were few roads. Sometimes, the telephone was more reliable than the postal service in these places.

As a true visionary hero, Alexander Graham Bell knew that the possibilities that the telephone created were nearly limitless. In an accurate view of the future, Bell once even said:

> *"The day will come when the man at the telephone will be able to see the distant person to whom he is speaking."*

Alexander Graham Bell wouldn't be surprised if he were here today watching everyone buried in their cellphones, and he probably wouldn't be bothered by it. After all, from the time he was a child, Alexander Graham Bell set out to connect the world with his technology, and that is exactly what we are doing on our cellphones every day.

DID YOU KNOW?

- Bell was given no middle name at birth. He adopted the name Graham at age 11 out of respect for a family friend.

- Alexander married Mabel Hubbard in 1877 in Cambridge, Massachusetts. The couple had four children, but only two survived birth.

- Although Bell is known as a great American inventor and hero, he was born a British citizen and never gave up that status. He became a naturalized American citizen in 1882. Canada also claims him as one of their heroes, as he kept residences in Canada and the United States for most of his adult life.

- Bell was a bit of a philosopher known for many aphorisms, such as: *"When one door closes another opens"*; *"Preparation is the key to success"*; and *"A man is what he makes of himself."*

- Bell died on August 2, 1922 in Beinn Bhreagh, Nova Scotia at the age of 75 from complications due to diabetes.

GEORGE S. PATTON
AMERICA'S GREATEST WAR HERO

The United States doesn't have a particularly long history, relatively speaking. It may seem like 240 plus years is a long time, but when you compare that to some countries in Europe and Asia, it is a blip on the radar. When you take that and combine it with the fact that the United States has only been invaded once in that history, it stands to reason that this a country without many war heroes.

Many people would say that it's a good thing that there aren't many American war heroes. War is awful and far from being a glorious thing, but at the same time, it is sometimes impossible to avoid. And when you have to go to war, you need to have the best people possible to lead you.

General George S. Patton was probably the best American, of any period in history, to lead this nation in war. He was brash to the point of being obnoxious, and he loved war. It would be difficult to imagine Patton doing anything other than fighting wars.

When it came down to it, though, Patton was effective on the battlefield, commanded respect from friend and foe, and represented his country with honor.

Among the few war heroes that the United States has, General Patton has to be considered at the top of any list.

A BORN SOLDIER

Some people are just born for the military and seem destined to lead men into battle. Patton is one of those people, although the road was not always easy. The future four-star general was born George Smith Patton Jr. on November 11, 1885, in San Gabriel, California to George Sr. and Ruth Patton.

The military was certainly in Patton's blood, as he was descended from a long line of military officers and could claim lineage to notables who fought in several major wars, including the English Civil War, the American Revolution, and the American Civil War.

But as illustrious as Patton's military pedigree may have been, he almost didn't become an officer.

Young Patton had everything in his favor to become a military officer—his family was well-connected in military circles and he had a deep interest in the military—but he was not much of a student. He had a difficult time reading and writing, leading some historians to believe that he had the learning disability dyslexia long before it would have been routinely diagnosed.

Eventually, George Senior arranged for tutors to help his son, which seemed to help get him through the critical, formative years. George Junior eventually developed a love for reading everything military, and he especially loved to learn about all the great generals of world history.

George Junior's overwhelming desire was to join Pericles, Alexander the Great, and Robert E. Lee in immortality as one of the greatest generals in history.

George studied long hours and, with the help of his family connections, was admitted to the prestigious Virginia Military Institute (VMI). After being enrolled for only a year at VMI, though, an opportunity came knocking when he was nominated to attend West Point by a California senator.

West Point was surely Patton's first major step toward military leadership, but he had to pass the classes first, which he found extremely difficult due to his learning disabilities.

After having to repeat his first year of studies due to poor grades, George settled down and began doing better in his course work. He proved to be a natural leader among his classmates and was a true jock, participating in several organized sports.

Patton was such a good athlete that he even participated in the 1912 Summer Olympics in the pentathlon!

George graduated from West Point in 1909 in the middle of his class, which was more than respectable considering his challenges. But Patton was happy to be done with scholarship; the only way he was going to prove himself to his warrior ancestors was on the battlefield.

A NEW TYPE OF WARFARE

Like any person of destiny, Patton always seemed to end up in the right place at the right time. After graduating from West Point, Patton was assigned to the cavalry as an officer.

Back in those days, the cavalry still rode horses, although that was all about to change. But before that would happen, Patton had the opportunity to take part in one of the more interesting episodes in American history.

From 1910 to 1920, Mexico was embroiled in a revolution. The situation spilled over into the American state of New Mexico in late 1915 and early 1916. The United States responded by sending General John *"Blackjack"* Pershing to invade Mexico and capture rebel leader Pancho Villa. At Pershing's side as his aid was Patton. Although the Americans never captured Villa, Patton was able to experience combat for the first time, and it was something that he loved.

More important than the combat experience he gained, Patton impressed General Pershing. Unlike many of Patton's teachers early in his life, Pershing saw a certain brightness in the young officer.

When the United States entered World War I in 1917, Pershing brought Patton with him as his aid and taught the young man even more about the military. The two men were of a like mind, at least militarily speaking, as both Pershing and Patton knew that traditional cavalry was a thing of the past and that armored warfare/tanks were the future.

Patton showed great aptitude for armored warfare and was assigned to teach tank tactics to Allied soldiers before he was assigned to lead a tank brigade on the final Allied offensive of the war, in the fall of 1918.

Patton earned his brash reputation in the offensive, often riding on top of his tank, urging his men to charge. Although he was shot during one battle, he kept fighting and even claimed to have assaulted one of his men who wouldn't charge forward.

World War I cemented Patton's reputation as a leader and earned him steady promotions in rank. The conflict also proved that tanks were the future of warfare; Patton would play a central role in America's use of the new weapons.

OLD BLOOD AND GUTS

Patton found the interwar years incredibly difficult. He wanted nothing more than to fight in another war and hated being cooped up in offices or leading endless drills. He often butted heads with his superior officers, which made getting peacetime promotions nearly impossible.

But when World War II began in 1939, Patton's fortunes changed once more. The American high-command watched in awe and horror as the German Army, led by their tanks, blazed a path of destruction across Europe and North Africa.

The Americans knew that it was only a matter of time before they were pulled into the war and that the best chance, they had of winning was to fight fire with fire. The only way to beat the seemingly invincible German tank commander Rommel was to throw their tank commander at him.

Patton was promoted to general and given a key role in the invasion of North Africa — codenamed Operation Torch — in November 1942.

Almost immediately, Patton began blazing a path of destruction of his own across North Africa, sending the Germans and Italians back to Italy. Patton then worked his way up Italy, scoring victory after victory along the way. General Eisenhower then reassigned Patton to play a key role in the liberation of France in 1944. He later helped stop the German counteroffensive at the Battle of the Bulge in the winter of 1944–45.

As Patton scored victory after victory, he became a hero to the American people back home and to the rank-and-file of his troops, who began referring to him as *"old blood and guts"* for his fearless, no-nonsense attitude. Yet he was still often an outsider among the military brass, who often didn't like his attitude.

He slapped two privates in Sicily in 1943, accusing them of cowardice, but the incidents were overlooked by Eisenhower because, by then, he was the most effective on-the-ground American general. Other incidents followed, which were compounded by his often politically incorrect statements to the press.

Once the war was over, Patton was assigned a peacetime role of rebuilding Europe. Unlike the polished Eisenhower, Patton never measured his statements and often offended powerful people in the process. He was critical of the Soviet Union and the Russian people and he publicly compared the Nazis to Republicans and Democrats, as just another political party.

This was all too much for Eisenhower. Patton was relieved of his command in September 1945.

The old war hero didn't live much longer, dying from injuries sustained in a car accident in Germany on December 8, 1945. He died in a hospital in Heidelberg on December 21, 1945 at the age of 60.

AMERICA'S GENERAL

Patton's status as America's greatest war hero was cemented while he was still alive. Americans kept abreast of his many victories in North Africa and Europe through newspapers and films. When Patton briefly returned to the United States in June 1945, he was met with throngs of spectators.

He did a whirlwind tour of American cities, visiting Los Angeles, Boston, Denver, and Washington. He even managed to pull more than 100,000 spectators into the Los Angeles Coliseum to hear him speak. The USC Trojans could only wish to get that type of a crowd!

There is little doubt that Patton could've carried his immense popularity into politics had he not died. Rather than Eisenhower, it could have been Patton who became president. Instead, Patton is remembered as a skilled tactician with an often acerbic personality. Americans love a winner, but they also love a guy who is willing to speak his mind, so for those reasons, George S. Patton will always be remembered as America's top general.

DID YOU KNOW?

- Patton desperately wanted to be sent to the Pacific after the war in Europe had ended but was made military governor of Bavaria instead. He felt that his talents were wasted in the largely political role.

- Patton's body is interred at the American Cemetery and Memorial in Luxembourg City, Luxembourg.

- He married Beatrice Banning Ayer in 1910. The couple had two daughters and one son. Their son, George S. Patton IV, rose to the rank of general in the army.

- Patton was an accomplished fencer and polo player. He suffered a serious injury in a 1936 polo match.

- Patton commanded the Third Army in Europe. Although the Third Army was not involved in the actual Normandy Invasion, it drove through France and the Low Countries and later occupied Germany.

MARTIN LUTHER
KING JUNIOR
FIGHTING FOR CIVIL RIGHTS

We've seen in our book that many American heroes never carried a gun. These men and women became heroes through, by, and for peaceful methods. Whether they invented devices that helped humanity or enlightened us with their knowledge, there have been plenty of peaceful American heroes. And when the subject of peaceful American heroes is brought up, Martin Luther King Jr. is often the first person who comes to mind.

There is little doubt that Martin Luther King Jr. fundamentally transformed the United States of America. The term *"civil rights"* is directly associated with him, as he worked nonstop to end racial discrimination in America and, ultimately, opened the door for other groups to assert their rights.

You may find it hard to believe, but while Martin Luther King Jr. was alive, he was somewhat of a polarizing figure. Yes, many people loved the man and what he stood for, yet there were still many who violently opposed him.

Even those who supported his message often thought that he was pushing for too much too soon. They didn't think

America was ready for his ideas. In some ways, you could say those people were right, as King's life ended in a tragic assassination.

Today, Martin Luther King Jr. has a federal holiday and is regarded as a hero by a large segment of Americans from all backgrounds.

A DIFFERENT AMERICA

To understand how and why Martin Luther King Jr. became an American hero, it is important to understand the America into which he was born. King was born Michael King Jr. on January 15, 1929 in Atlanta, Georgia to Baptist minister Michael King Senior and his wife, Alberta. It was the era known as Jim Crow in the United States, when racial segregation and discrimination were legal, especially in the Southern states.

You're probably wondering if his father was named Michael King Senior, how did Martin Luther King Jr. get his name? Well, King Senior embarked on a trip in 1934 that brought him to the Middle East and Europe. While in Germany, he became impressed with the story of the great Protestant reformer, Martin Luther, who risked his life for his faith. When King Senior returned to America, he changed his and his son's names to reflect his spiritual experience.

Despite growing up in an era of legal discrimination against Blacks, Martin was part of a stable, middle-class family. King Senior was a successful pastor of Ebenezer Baptist Church in Atlanta, so he was able to provide for his family materially and spiritually. Junior and his two younger siblings grew up reading Bible verses and learning about the realities of life in

America. Although the Kings were materially better off than nearly all of their neighbors—and even many Whites for that matter—doors were still closed to them. Junior watched as his father led protests against discrimination in the Atlanta area, which is where he first learned about organizing and fighting the system through peaceful means.

Although today Atlanta is a predominantly African American city, it wasn't in the 1930s. The Black population, though, was still quite large. Yet, due to the legal system of segregation, the city's Black children had only one high school they could attend—Booker T. Washington. But Martin didn't let the limitations impede his academic success. He was consistently at the top of his class and even skipped a grade. He showed a special aptitude for oratory at a young age, which he would use extensively throughout his career as a minister and civil rights hero.

King entered the historically Black Morehouse College in Atlanta at the age of 15, quickly learning that, although he may have been the top student in his high school class, things were different in college. Although he never distinguished himself at Morehouse, earning average marks, he persevered and earned a BA in 1948. King then earned a divinity degree from Crozer Theological Seminary in Pennsylvania in 1951 and a Ph.D. in theology from Boston University in 1954.

That was also the same year that he became pastor of the Dexter Avenue Baptist Church in Montgomery, Alabama. It was while in this position that King launched his career as a civil rights hero, forever changing the United States.

A CIVIL RIGHTS ICON

King's first true battle as a civil rights hero came in late 1955. The public transportation in Montgomery, Alabama — and throughout most of the South — was segregated, with Black riders being forced to sit in the back. If the bus filled up, White riders could force the Black riders to stand. On December 1, 1955, another civil rights icon, Rosa Parks, decided not to give her seat up to a White rider, which resulted in her arrest and protests from the city's Black community.

At the front of the Montgomery Bus Boycott was Martin Luther King Jr. King and other local Black leaders urged the city's Black community to find other modes of transportation until the city's policy of segregated seating ended. An attempt was made on King's life and he was briefly held in jail for his leadership role in the boycott, but he was victorious in the end. The United States Supreme Court overturned the racial segregation policy on the Montgomery public transit system, which established King as the de facto leader of the American civil rights movement.

The victory also made King plenty of enemies.

MARCHING TO WASHINGTON

King took his message across the South throughout the late 1950s and early 1960s. He faced assault and more arrests, but he persisted. As the leader of the Southern Christian Leadership Conference (SCLC), King became the most recognized civil rights leader in America and, arguably, the world. He met with presidents Kennedy and Johnson as well several leaders from both major American political parties.

The connections King made within the civil rights movement and the government culminated in the August 28, 1963 March on Washington for Jobs and Freedom. Although King was not the primary organizer of the event, his *"I Have a Dream"* speech captured the imagination of the nearly 300,000 in attendance, and the television cameras there made sure that his words would be immortalized.

Almost as soon as he gave the speech, changes took place.

Congress passed and President Lyndon Johnson signed the Civil Rights Act of 1964, which outlawed racial segregation and discrimination. A year later, the Voting Rights Act of 1965 was passed, allowing millions of Blacks in the South to vote for the first time in their lives.

King had already been a hero to Black Americans for many years, but people around the world were beginning to recognize the man for his achievements by the mid-1960s. He was awarded the prestigious Nobel Peace Prize in 1964 and his media profile was continually increasing in the United States.

By the late 1960s, things had changed again in America. Many of the reforms that King had fought for were achieved, but the country was embroiled in the Vietnam War, which threatened to tear the country apart from within. Martin Luther King Jr. stood against the Vietnam War, but he did so without disparaging American servicemen and women. It was a war that he opposed on moral grounds in a nonviolent manner, as he did during his long struggle in the civil rights movement.

When Martin Luther King Jr. was assassinated in Memphis, Tennessee on April 4, 1968, many thought that the assassin had killed King's dream. Those closest to him knew that, in many ways, it had already come true.

A HERO FOR HIS TIME

There's no telling what Martin Luther King Jr. would've done if he had lived a longer life. What is certain, though, is that he was the right kind of hero for the time. Martin Luther King Jr. brought his mission to the mostly poor Blacks of the South when they had few resources or people to stand up for them. He gave those people something to believe in and hope that not just their lives, but also the lives of their children and grandchildren, would be better.

Hope is one of the most powerful and positive of all human emotions. If anyone can add so much hope to the world, then surely, he has to be a hero, right?

DID YOU KNOW?

- Martin Luther King Jr. is often known today by the abbreviation MLK. MLK married his only wife, Coretta Scott, in 1953. They had four children.

- MLK's body was interred in the Martin Luther King Jr. National Historic Park. The park consists of King's grave, his boyhood home, the Ebenezer Baptist Church, and a museum.

- Although MLK's birthday is on January 15th, MLK Day, which is the national holiday that celebrates his life, is on the third Monday of January, so the date varies each year.

- It may not seem important that King chose nonviolent methods to pursue his ideas, but in the 1960s, many Black leaders and organizations—such as Malcolm X and the Black Panthers—were openly calling for violent revolution. King was derided by some of these groups as an *"Uncle Tom."*

- King was greatly influenced by the nonviolent tactics of Indian leader Mohandas Gandhi. Both leaders were assassinated by those who opposed their ideas.

ELVIS PRESLEY
PIONEERING AMERICA'S ENTERTAINMENT INDUSTRY

When you talk about the evolution of the American entertainment industry, one name usually comes to mind — Elvis Presley. Elvis was truly a man ahead of his time, an entertainment visionary and, to many people all over the world, a true American hero.

If you think about everything Elvis did in his relatively short life, it's hard to deny his hero status. Elvis was arguably the world's first rock star, scoring hit after hit on the charts and playing to packed houses. He was one of the first musicians to effectively use the medium of television.

Elvis was also the first mass media rebel, angering American parents over his gyrations on stage, his clothing, his hairstyles, and his devil may care attitude. Boys wanted to be like him, and girls wanted to be with him.

And just like a true rebel and trailblazer, Elvis was the first entertainer to go by just one name.

But Elvis Presley was much more than just a rebellious rock 'n' roller. He was a talented musician who could play multiple instruments and was just as accomplished at recording gospel and country music. Elvis was also one of the first major musicians to try his hand at acting, although most of his films bordered on camp.

There is no denying that Elvis Presley touched a lot of people's hearts and became the voice of a generation. Despite now being dead for more than 40 years, Elvis' memory lives on in the hearts of legions of fans of all backgrounds and ages—just go to Graceland during Elvis Week in Memphis, Tennessee to see for yourself.

A STAR IS BORN

It's said that you can only know the blues if you've experienced true adversity in your life. Well, Elvis Aaron Presley inherited the blues, as he was born into poverty on January 8, 1935, in Tupelo, Mississippi. To make things more difficult, Elvis was a twin, but his brother, Jesse, was delivered 35 minutes before Elvis, stillborn.

The death of Elvis' twin would affect him throughout his life. He claimed to have a mystical connection with his brother, and he dedicated his career to him.

But before he could become famous, Elvis had to deal with poverty.

Elvis' parents, Vernon and Gladys, gave him a stable home, but money was scarce. Elvis was born during the Great Depression and things were particularly tough in the South and in the small town of Tupelo, so the Presley family moved to nearby Memphis, Tennessee in 1948.

Things weren't a whole lot better in Memphis. Vernon found more work, but the cost of living was much higher, forcing the family to live in public housing. By that time, though, Elvis had blossomed into a young musician. He learned gospel in church and from his family and picked up country music from his family and friends.

But he was most impressed by the blues.

Any chance he could get, Elvis would go down to the Beale Street neighborhood to watch street musicians play the blues. Beale Street is the historic business district of Memphis' Black community. At that time, it was filled with a combination of lawyer, doctor, and dentist offices, as well as bars and juke joints. Elvis made plenty of contacts on Beale Street, which included legendary bluesmen like B.B. King, and began making a name for himself.

Elvis also began cultivating his style in the early 1950s, adopting a *"greaser"* look with Vaseline slicked hair, wingtip shoes, and flashy shirts.

By the time Elvis graduated high school in 1953, it was clear to many — including him — that a star had been born in Memphis, Tennessee.

BECOMING AN AMERICAN ICON

When Elvis walked into Sun Studios in Memphis to record a demo in August 1953, no one in the studio knew who he was. After he left, it was assured that his name would never be forgotten. Record producer Sam Phillips knew that Elvis was special.

He was a talented musician who could seamlessly blend two uniquely American music styles — country and blues — in a way that didn't seem possible. Remember, 1950s America was quite segregated, especially in the South, and this extended to music: country was *"White"* music and blues was *"Black"* music.

Elvis' music style, which became known as rockabilly, became quite popular as he toured the South. He was eventually signed to RCA records.

But Elvis' good looks helped him transcend the music industry to become a true cultural icon.

By the mid-1950s, a large number of Americans had televisions in their homes, and those who didn't knew a relative or neighbor with one. Elvis began making television appearances on the *Ed Sullivan Show* and other similar variety shows, where he caused a stir by gyrating his pelvis as he sang. Although there were calls to make sure he was never on TV again, the kids loved him, and his popularity grew.

By 1958, Elvis was a legend in his own time.

But the legend almost came to an end when Elvis was drafted into the U.S. Army and stationed in West Germany in 1958. Americans never forgot about Elvis during his two-year hitch in the Army, thanks in part to singles he recorded that were released while he was serving. The absence only seemed to make the public crave Elvis more.

In the 1960s, Elvis leapt from recording artist to actor. Today, that transition is done quite regularly, but in the early 1960s, Elvis was the first notable personality to make the move. He starred in dozens of movies in the '60s, including *Blue Hawaii*, *Girls! Girls! Girls!*, and *Viva Las Vegas*.

By the late 1960s, Elvis' old style was viewed as a bit corny by the new youth generation, so he reinvented himself to appeal to a wider audience. The new image proved to be successful, sending Elvis to the top of the charts again. He totaled more than 115 *Billboard* top 40 hits in his career, which is a record that will probably never be beaten.

A TRAGIC HERO

Though an American hero, Elvis was also a tragic one. In an era when music icons were a new concept—never mind the multi-faceted entertainment icon that he was—Elvis never really knew how to handle the success.

The reality was that, even when Elvis Presley was at the top of his game in the early 1960s, he was still a mama's boy from Memphis, Tennessee. His good, trusting nature is part of what made him so beloved by so many, but it also proved to be his demise. Elvis put his trust in too many untrustworthy people. The people who cared about him were often pushed aside by those who only wanted to profit from his fame.

By the early 1970s, Elvis had developed addictions to numerous prescription pills and also eating disorders, which left him obese and often barely able to perform live. Needless to say, he was a shadow of his former self. On August 16, 1977, Elvis died of a heart attack that was the result of his health problems. He was only 42 years old.

Millions of fans mourned the passing of America's first true entertainment icon. His legendary status has only seemed to grow in the decades since his death. Elvis is still the most recognizable name in American pop culture history, as he continues to exert influence on the cultural landscape. Elvis

143

Presley touched so many lives in his short time on Earth, which makes him a true American hero.

DID YOU KNOW?

- Beginning in grade school, Elvis often carried a guitar with him wherever he went. Many of his schoolmates would make fun of him for his guitar, causing Elvis to become somewhat of a loner during his school years. I guess he had the last laugh, right?

- Elvis' long-time business manager was Thomas *"Colonel Tom"* Parker. Parker was Dutch-born and was rumored not to have legal residency status in the United States. Many believe this is why Canada was the only country Elvis toured outside of the U.S.

- Due to his hip gyrating dance, Elvis was known as Elvis the Pelvis in his early years of fame, although his most enduring nickname is The King.

- Elvis married Priscilla in 1967 after meeting her while he was in the Army. The couple had one child, Lisa Marie.

- Besides B.B. King, Elvis played with and befriended many other giants of American blues and country music, including Johnny Cash, Jerry Lee Lewis, and Ike Turner.

GEORGE WASHINGTON
AMERICA'S FIRST AND FOREMOST HERO

A book about great American heroes wouldn't be complete without a chapter dedicated to the first hero, George Washington. Even Americans who are extremely lacking in knowledge of their country's history know a little about Washington. Most can say with confidence that he was the United States' first president.

Plus, there are plenty of reminders of Washington's greatness, in case you somehow forget about his role in this nation's creation. There is the Washington monument in the capital city of the United States, which bears the man's name, Washington! And, of course, Washington's image adorns the most common paper currency bill in the United States and also the 25-cent coin.

Washington's image has also been on numerous stamps. He has had colleges and cities named after him and even one state. Truly, you don't have to look far to find George Washington's influence in the United States. It is equally clear that the American people still venerate the first president.

And a brief look at Washington's life shows that he deserves that veneration.

Although born to privilege, Washington never used his position, as many would've at the time. Instead, he proved himself among his peers and the American people through action and deeds. He rose through the ranks of the Colonial American Army to become the commander-in-chief of the Continental Army, where he led America to victory on the battlefield.

After America gained its independence, he became the first President of the United States of America. In a feat that has not since been replicated, he left office just as popular as when he was first elected. For his service on the battlefield and in the halls of government, George Washington earned the moniker, the Father of the Country, which makes him America's first hero.

A SON OF VIRGINIA

Washington was born on February 22, 1732 to a wealthy family in northern Virginia, which did not necessarily mean young George's life was easy. At that time, being wealthy in the American colonies was quite different to being wealthy in Britain—the colonists had to be much more self-sufficient and deal with privations every day.

Washington came from a fairly large family. His father, Augustine, had married George's mother, Mary, after his first wife died. There was a total of nine Washington siblings, which meant that, when Augustine died in 1743, oldest son Lawrence became the head of the house.

You could say that young George Washington grew up with a bit of a chip on his shoulder. His older brothers received formal, classical educations in England, while he was homeschooled in Virginia. With that said, his tutors were some of the best in the colonies and George did excel in his studies, especially mechanical and practical subjects.

Later in life, George always wanted to impress his intellectual peers, such as Jefferson, Madison, and Franklin, with his knowledge, although he was never quite the philosopher those men were.

Washington was never much of an orator, either. Yet he still commanded respect whenever he entered a room. At more than six-feet tall and over 200 pounds, Washington could be an intimidating physical presence. His size and manner would later help him in his military and political careers, but long before that, he planned to be just another Virginia plantation owner.

All of the young George's plans changed in 1751 when his brother Lawrence was suffering from tuberculosis. Although science had taken monumental leaps forward in the 1700s, antibiotic medicine was still quite a way in the future.

About the only thing that could be done for respiratory disease, such as tuberculosis, back then was for an afflicted person to move to a warmer climate. George and Lawrence moved to Barbados, but it was too little too late. Lawrence Washington died in 1752 and George contracted smallpox while on the Caribbean island.

The Barbados trip had long-lasting effects that stayed with George Washington for the rest of his life and shaped him into the man he became. Losing Lawrence, who was like a father to him, was truly tragic and, when combined with his bout of smallpox, made George realize just how tenuous life could be.

George Washington returned to Virginia with a new zest for life, determined to make something of himself.

THE MAKING OF A WARRIOR

Inspired by Lawrence's military service, George joined the Virginia militia in 1752 as an officer. Within two years he found himself right in the middle of the French and Indian War (1754–1763).

In May 1754, Washington led a force of about 300 Virginia militia into what is now Pennsylvania, where they ambushed and massacred a small French force. Washington later claimed that miscommunication led to the affair, but the French pointed out that all of their men were scalped by the Iroquois allies of the British. However, the massacre took place, it wasn't a good look for Washington and is considered the spark that set off the French and Indian War.

Washington's performance in the war was further complicated when he was forced to surrender Fort Necessity, but by the end of the war he grew into a capable commander. Most importantly, Washington learned how to fight on the unique American terrain during the French and Indian War. He also made some important contacts.

After the French and Indian War, Washington used those connections to move up in life and raise his political profile.

AMERICA'S FIRST LEADER

In the years after the French and Indian War, Washington married, became even richer by acquiring more land and slaves, and entered politics. He was elected to the Virginia

House of Burgesses in 1758, which was Virginia's representative assembly. While in the House, Washington railed against British taxes and British soldiers on American soil, eventually becoming one of the primary Patriot leaders from Virginia.

Washington may not have been as articulate or erudite as other notables from Virginia, such as Jefferson and Madison, but he was more charismatic.

After the colonies established the Continental Congress, Washington was elected as Virginia's representative, but it wasn't long before destiny had other ideas.

The Continental Congress voted to make George Washington the commander-in-chief of the Continental Army in 1775. It may have been a nice title, but it was certainly no easy task. Washington was up against the best equipped and most professional army in the world.

On the other hand, he commanded an army of farmers who received little pay throughout the war. Washington himself received little pay and at times considered selling his plantation, Mount Vernon, in Virginia to pay for the war effort.

But Washington only needed to *survive*; at least, that was his strategy. He knew that it would be difficult to decisively defeat the British on the battlefield, so his strategy was simply to keep the Continental Army together and to pull off a few victories if possible.

After losing some important early battles that cost him New York, Washington crossed the Delaware River and defeated a Hessian force in New Jersey on December 26, 1776. His troops then fought the British to a standstill in June 1778. It wasn't enough to beat the British, but it was enough to bring the French into the war on America's side.

Washington then led the allied American and French forces at the Battle of Yorktown in 1781, which ensured American independence.

George Washington proved himself as a true American hero on the battlefield during the American Revolution, but it was after the war that he established himself as a hero in peacetime.

The nature of the United States government after the war was a problem, to say the least. It was essentially 13 separate countries that had no way to protect its borders, and they were often at each other's throats.

James Madison, Alexander Hamilton, and others believed that the states could only be united through a central government, as outlined in the United States Constitution. Passing the Constitution, though, would not be easy.

Each state would have to give up some power to join the federation, so the pro-Constitution forces enlisted Washington to go to Philadelphia as an advocate of the new government. Washington's presence at the Constitutional Convention of 1787 was vital for the passage of the Constitution and the unification of the states under one government.

Washington then planned to go back to Mount Virginia and retire, but duty called once more. The same guys who drafted George Washington to be the face of the United States Constitution thought that he should be the first president of the new government and nation!

There were no political parties or conventions as there are today — Washington's name was simply added to the ballot with a host of others. And the election took forever! Due to the slow pace of travel (remember, this was before phones, television, radio, or cars) the actual election (not the campaign) began on December 15, 1788 and ended on January 10, 1789.

The results were never in question.

Washington won all 69 electoral votes in a landslide and was reelected in 1792 in a similar landslide.

In an era when the people still genuinely trusted and — in Washington's case — loved their leaders, the presidency of George Washington was free from scandal and major partisan conflicts. Yes, there were partisan conflicts within the government and even Washington's cabinet, and the first political parties formed during his presidency, but he was truly a unifying figure for the country.

At a time when the new country was weak in many ways, internally and externally, Washington brought Americans together and projected an image of strength to the outside world. It was what America needed to survive its first few tenuous years of existence.

THE FIRST UNIFIER

When you consider what made George Washington a hero, it is difficult to point to just one thing. He was America's first general and the nation's first president. Of course, he had his foibles: he was a slave owner and was often uncompromising and difficult to deal with.

With that said, he freed most of his slaves before he died in 1799, and his wife later freed the remaining slaves on their Mount Vernon plantation. And, in terms of his uncompromising nature, it was an asset one needed in those days—it was a tougher time, when duels were accepted practice. Having a sharp tongue sometimes came in handy!

Yes, George Washington was a complex man and a man of his time. The contributions he made to the foundation of the United States of America are immeasurable and are still seen and felt today. Because of those contributions, George Washington is not only the father of this country but also America's first presidential hero.

DID YOU KNOW?

- Washington died on December 14, 1799 at his plantation in Mount Vernon, Virginia at the age of 67. The exact cause of Washington's death remains a mystery, although it was probably some sort of tracheal infection that was possibly aggravated by a blood-letting treatment.

- George married Martha in 1759. She was a widower with two children, John and Martha Parke, whom George raised as children of his own. The couple never had children together, which has been the cause of much historical speculation.

- Since Washington is such a revered figure in American history, many myths and legends have developed about his life. It is commonly repeated that Washington had wooden teeth. Although he did have *false* teeth, they weren't wooden. The story of him cutting down his family's cherry tree is also probably a legend since little is known about his childhood.

- George Washington was a Freemason, as were many of the Founding Fathers.

- Washington was opposed to the formation of political parties, fearing that they would tear the United States apart. Despite Washington's opposition, the opposing Federalist and Democratic–Republican parties formed during his second term as president.

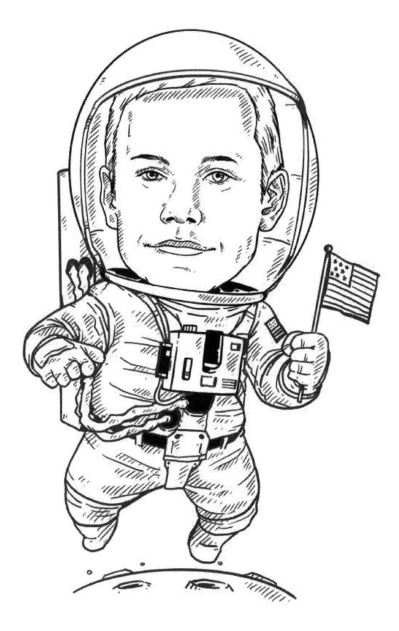

NEIL ARMSTRONG
"ONE GIANT LEAP FOR MANKIND"

Ever since the dawn of humanity, people have looked to the sky and beyond for inspiration. The Sun, the Moon, and the planets are always in the sky for people to see, but the very nature of the celestial bodies eluded humans for millennia. Were the stars holes in the sky? Were the planets just gas clouds? How far away were the planets? Was the Earth flat? And of course: was the Earth in the middle of it all?

As human knowledge progressed, many of these questions began to be answered. The Greeks determined that Earth is a sphere, as indicated by maps made by the 2nd century AD geographer, Ptolemy. In the 16th century, Copernicus proved that the Sun was the center of our solar system and Isaac Newton proved the theory of gravity in the 17th century.

All of these men were great scientific heroes to whom we owe an immense debt of gratitude. They paved the way for the creation of the modern world and opened the door for later heroes to take their ideas to the next level. Heroes like Neil Armstrong, who took their ideas to the Moon.

Neil Armstrong became one of the most beloved American heroes when he stated the now-famous words, *"That's one small step for man, one giant leap for mankind."*

Armstrong didn't just make a leap forward for Americans, but for everyone on this planet. He was the first human to touch down on a non-Earth surface, making him the greatest explorer of the 20th century and one of the most admired Americans of all time.

STARING AT THE SKY

When Neil Armstrong was a young boy growing up in Ohio in the 1930s, he looked to the skies for inspiration. He first flew in an airplane with his father when he was six and, by his teens, he had earned a student pilot certificate.

Neil excelled in his classes and showed a particular aptitude for science and math. It was clear to Neil's family that his life would take him far beyond their working-class Midwest background, but just how far, no one knew.

Well, maybe Neil Armstrong himself knew.

Neil was a noticeably confident young man, although he was never arrogant and usually quite reserved. He planned a course for his life that involved a career in aviation, which would mean that he needed to attend college.

No one in the Armstrong family had attended college, so young Neil began his career as a trailblazer when he entered Purdue University in 1947. To pay for his tuition, Armstrong enrolled in the Holloway Plan, which paid for his tuition in return for military service.

Armstrong entered the Navy in 1949 and, in 1951, at the age of 21, he was sent to the Korean War. It was while he was in Korea that Armstrong acquired valuable experience that he would use when he became a legendary astronaut.

Armstrong flew 78 bombing missions in one of the first jet planes to be based on an aircraft carrier, the Grumman F9F Panther. The experience put him ahead of many pilots and astronauts of the era and also introduced him to some of the important people he would later work with at NASA.

After his service, he returned to Purdue, graduated, and started a family. But Neil Armstrong wasn't about to settle down. There was a galaxy out there to be explored and Armstrong would be the man to lead the way!

A SPACE AGE EXPLORER

Neil Armstrong entered NASA in 1962, at just the right time in history. The Soviet Union was leading the so-called space race at that point: they had launched the first artificial satellite in 1957, put the first animal in space in 1957, and launched the first human into space in 1961.

All of this happened in the middle of the Cold War, which frightened the American people, causing American politicians to react. U.S. President John F. Kennedy's response was to put the first man on the Moon.

The long-term mission of putting a man on the Moon became known as the Apollo Mission. Neil Armstrong would be at the center of the Apollo Mission from the beginning, and despite it being a success, it was a difficult and often dangerous road.

Although Armstrong was a former Navy pilot, he was a civilian when he entered NASA and was the first of two civilian astronauts, along with Elliot See. The training was rigorous and meant to push the astronauts to their limits.

They were placed in zero gravity for long periods, given strict diets, and expected to learn the intricacies of complex machines very quickly. Armstrong excelled in all the tests and so was picked to become the first American civilian to go into space. He flew in the Gemini VIII capsule for ten hours above Earth.

Armstrong would orbit around the earth several more times in other Gemini missions, which made him a household name in America. His fame brought him into elevated circles with presidents and other high-ranking politicians, as well as dignitaries, movie stars, and influential people from around the world.

But the fame never really got to Neil. He was still the same humble guy from the Midwest, preferring to spend time with his family over parties with big wigs. He was never too stuck-up to sign an autograph.

The Gemini missions also prepared Armstrong for entry into the Apollo Program, since the Gemini crafts would be similar to those used to get to the Moon. But the Apollo Program was almost over before it started.

On January 27, 1967, tragedy struck when the Apollo 1 burst into flames during a rehearsed takeoff in Cape Canaveral, Florida, killing all three astronauts on board.

The tragedy only seemed to steel Armstrong's resolve, though. He never wavered from his goal to walk on the Moon and was rewarded for his hard work by being given back-up command of Apollo 8. The Apollo astronauts were routinely rotated through crews and missions, which resulted in Armstrong earning another promotion — and his ultimate date with destiny — commander of the Apollo 11 mission.

When asked by reporters why the Apollo Mission was needed, Armstrong replied, in true explorer fashion, *"We're going to the Moon because it's in the nature of the human being."*

Ferdinand Magellan, Marco Polo, or Lewis and Clark couldn't have said it any better.

After other Apollo missions paved the way by successfully orbiting the Moon, the green light was given to Apollo 11 to fly to and land on the Moon. On July 16, 1969, Armstrong, Buzz Aldrin, and Michael Collins blasted off from the Kennedy Space Center in Florida in a Saturn V rocket. Four days later, they arrived at their destination.

When Armstrong bounced out of his craft and looked at the Earth, he put everything in perspective, later saying, *"I put up my thumb and it blotted out the Earth."*

Needless to say, when the Apollo 11 crew returned to Earth days later, everything had changed.

PUTTING THE WORLD INTO PERSPECTIVE

After his work with the Apollo Mission, Armstrong continued to lead a very fulfilling life. He taught aeronautics at the University of Cincinnati, was a successful businessman, and even went to the North Pole on an expedition in 1985.

Ever a humble guy, Neil never really liked being called a hero. He never really fit in with the D.C. elite crowds and shied away from politics as much as possible. He never made his political affiliation explicitly known, if he even had one, which probably endeared him even more to the American people.

When all of Neil Armstrong's life is considered, he was an

everyman hero. He was a hard-working guy from a solid family who earned everything he got in life. A true American pioneer and explorer, Neil Armstrong pushed the limits of human capacity and came out as the victor.

Neil Armstrong is often thought of as a great American hero for being the first man on the Moon, which is certainly enough to make him one. However, it was the example he set throughout his life and the type of man he was that truly make him one of the greatest American heroes.

DID YOU KNOW?

- Armstrong married his first wife, Janet, in 1956. They had three children. Neil and Janet divorced in 1994 and he married Carol Knight that same year.

- Armstrong earned a Master of Science degree from the University of Southern California in 1970. The degree was in aerospace engineering through USC's Viterbi School of Engineering.

- Immediately after graduating from Purdue, Neil worked as a test pilot and was involved in several near-death experiences.

- Armstrong and Aldrin landed on the Moon in a craft known as the Eagle. Aldrin joined Armstrong after about 20 minutes and the two then collected samples for about two hours. They stayed on the Eagle for about 20 hours before lifting off and rendezvousing with Collins.

- The Moon landing was—and arguably remains—the greatest moment in television history. Thanks to state-of-the-art cameras NASA placed on the Eagle, viewers back on Earth were able to watch it all live.

MARK TWAIN
THE GREATEST AMERICAN AUTHOR

A really good writer defines their generation. Jack Kerouac was said to have defined the Beat Generation with his stories that chronicled life as an itinerant in the United States, in books such as *On the Road* and *The Dharma Bums.*

Kerouac's writings had an immense impact on the youth culture of the time and continue to be a favorite among younger people, but his works are somewhat niche.

Defining a generation is no easy thing, which is why writers like Kerouac don't come around very often. Generation-defining authors are skilled and unique in their approach to the craft, but as good as they are, only a few of them can also define their people or an entire era.

This rarest category of writers is reserved for such luminaries as Johann Wolfgang von Goethe, who captured the spirit of Germany in the 19th century, and Charles Dickens, who will forever be remembered as a part of Victorian England.

Writers like Goethe and Dickens were not simply great writers who brought the struggles and feelings of their people to life through their pens, they eventually became true heroes in their countries' cultural landscapes.

The American people have their own, similar literary hero—Mark Twain.

Unless you've been living under a rock, if you're an American, you know a little bit about Mark Twain, the pen name of 19th-century writer Samuel Clemens. He wrote such widely read and influential books as *The Adventures of Tom Sawyer* and *The Adventures of Huckleberry Finn*.

Twain also penned dozens of short stories, poems, and essays, traveled the world during an era when few went more than a couple of miles from their homes in the course of a lifetime, dined with dignitaries, and even piloted a Mississippi riverboat. Twain truly led an interesting life, which captured the American spirit of the pioneering 1800s and the American outlook on life in general.

When it comes to the American literary world, there is no doubt that Mark Twain sits far above all others and is a true American hero of the arts.

RIDING THE TAILS OF A COMET

Samuel Clemens' life began as Halley's Comet passed by the Earth on November 30, 1835. It was a sign of the life that the legendary American writer would lead—always on the move and full of energy, ready to bring his ideas and imagination to the public.

Although he was born in Florida, Clemens spent his formative years in Hannibal, Missouri. In Antebellum America, Hannibal was quite a bustling and important town.

Located close to the fertile agricultural areas of the Midwest, farmers often brought their goods to Hannibal to have them shipped down the river to New Orleans and beyond, or to the Ohio River where they would make their way east.

Like the true free spirit that he was, Clemens spent his time observing the many interesting folks he met in Hannibal, which he later used for grist for his best-known books.

Clemens learned about America, and life, from experience; he had little time for formal education and learned the tools of the writing trade while working for newspapers, magazines, and publishers in New York, Philadelphia, and St. Louis.

To further enhance his experiences, Clemens worked as a Mississippi River pilot in the years before the American Civil War. He was able to meet even more interesting people and see a different side of America he had never seen before, even though he grew up on the river.

It was during those years when Clemens learned that America was a unique place with a story waiting to be told and that American river culture was perhaps its most unique and fascinating aspect.

But before Sam could tell the story of America's Mississippi River culture, the country had to endure the Civil War.

The Civil War presented both challenges and opportunities for the young Clemens. Then in his mid-20s, Clemens was of fighting age for the war but would by no means be at the top of the draft. So, Sam decided to volunteer for a Confederate state militia.

Although Missouri was a slave state, it stayed in the Union during the Civil War. With that said, there was plenty of pro-Confederate sympathy in Missouri during the Civil War (remember Jesse James?) and young men who rallied to the South's cause.

Clemens wasn't a slave owner and Hannibal is located in the northeastern part of the state, across the river from Illinois and not far south of Iowa, yet he harbored slightly secessionist leanings.

Clemens also had a romantic notion of war that is common among many young men, writers especially. However, according to Clemens' account of his time in the war, he and most of the other men in his unit deserted in their first engagement with the enemy.

After just two weeks in the military, Samuel Clemens learned that he'd never be a soldier, so he packed up a few of his belongings and went to Nevada Territory to strike it rich.

MARK TWAIN IS BORN!

In 1861, Sam traveled with his brother Orion to the frontier of Nevada Territory. At that time, it was a place where you went to start over, make a fortune, or to find yourself. Samuel planned to do all three.

He was immediately impressed by the scenic beauty of the region and the rugged nature of the pioneers who chose to make it their home. He later recalled many of the people he met, things he saw, and adventures he had in some of his writings, but really what attracted him was the possibility of hitting it big.

Nevada was a booming territory after the discovery of the Comstock Lode brought tens of thousands of potential entrepreneurs to the region, hoping to find lodes of silver.

Clemens invested in and worked at several silver mines but never had any luck. After several months, it became clear to the starving artist that he just wasn't cut out to be a silver miner, or a miner of any type, for that matter. Lucky for Samuel Clemens, and the world, there were plenty of other opportunities in the Nevada Territory at the time.

Small mining camps became the boomtowns of Reno, Carson City, and Virginia City, which needed an entire infrastructure of workers to bring civilization to the frontier.

Clemens applied his loquacious pen to find a job writing a variety of articles for the Virginia City *Territorial Enterprise* under the pseudonym Josh. Clemens wrote about

scandals, shootouts, and whatever may have been interesting about and unique to frontier America, some of which he later used in his book *Roughing It*.

The job provided Clemens with a steady income doing something he enjoyed and, as he wrote to his sister, it came easy to him.

"They pay me six dollars a day," Clemens wrote his sister, *"and I make 50 per cent profit by only doing three dollars worth of work."*

It was when he was writing for the *Enterprise*, on February 3, 1863, that he began using his well-known pen name, Mark Twain. The precise reason why he chose the name remains unclear: it may be from the phrase Mississippi River boatmen sang out with their craft in two fathoms of water.

Others believe that it was coined in a Virginia City bar, where Clemens would request two shots whiskey and the bartenders would mark two chalk marks against his account on the back wall of the saloon.

Whatever the origin, Mark Twain was officially born in 1863 and never looked back. He went on to write for major newspapers and magazines and was sent on a tour of Europe and the Middle East.

After marrying and settling down in Connecticut, Twain was able to focus on the novels that made him famous. Using the vast knowledge he had acquired of the publishing industry, as well as countless connections, Twain published *The Adventures of Tom Sawyer* in 1876, *The Adventures of Huckleberry Finn* in 1884, and *A Connecticut Yankee in King Arthur's Court* in 1889, along with numerous other books, essays, short stories, and articles.

By the late 1800s, Mark Twain was not just a household name in America, he was known and loved throughout the world. His no-nonsense writing style and pragmatic world view made him the most recognizable American author of his time and since.

THE AMERICAN IMAGINATION

There is little doubt that Mark Twain is the best-known American writer of all time, which alone can qualify him as a hero. But perhaps most important is *what* and *how* he wrote. Twain came along at a time when Americans weren't known for producing any worthwhile literature or art.

Americans were respected and even praised by other people for their industriousness, efficiency, and ability to excel in business in the 1800s, but few thought any American could produce literature worthy of being read for decades, never mind centuries.

But that is exactly what Mark Twain did.

Twain proved that the American character can be both industrious and creative. Mark Twain never styled himself after better-known European writers, believing he would be untrue to himself if he did so, not to mention that it wouldn't sell to Americans. Ever the hardworking American, Twain worked until his death in 1910 and amassed a nice fortune in the process, but never sacrificed his art for money.

Mark Twain is a true hero of the arts, being the patron saint of American literature, proving that an American writer can be widely read more than 100 years after his death.

DID YOU KNOW?

- Twain is best known for his novels, but he was also a bit of a philosopher who loved to write aphorisms, some of which you've no doubt heard. *"Youth will come no more"*; *"There are basically two types of people. People who accomplish things, and people who claim to have accomplished things. The first group is less crowded"*; and *"Denial ain't just a river in Egypt"* are three of his better-known quotes.

- Twain married Olivia Langdon in 1870. She came from a wealthy, well-connected New England family. The couple had four children and, by all accounts, the marriage was quite happy.

- Although he made quite a bit of money from his writings, Twain was an otherwise poor businessman, which is perhaps a bit ironic when you consider that he embodied most other positive aspects of the American character. He was forced to file for bankruptcy in the 1800s.

- Throughout his life, Twain wore the big, bushy mustache for which he is known, although the accompanying white suit is more legend than fact.

- Mark Twain died on April 21, 1910, in Redding, Connecticut. He was buried next to his wife, who preceded him in death, in Elmira, New York.

SUSAN B. ANTHONY
BRINGING AMERICAN WOMEN
THE RIGHT TO VOTE

Long before Gloria Steinem and the modern feminist movement got underway in the 1960s and '70s, and even before the Nineteenth Amendment to the United States Constitution gave women the right to vote in 1920, Susan B. Anthony was fighting for equal rights for women, throughout much of the 1800s into the early 1900s.

Chances are you've heard the name Susan B. Anthony at some point in your life. You've probably even noticed her likeness on a dollar coin. But have you stopped to think about the impact she has had on the United States?

The reality is that Susan B. Anthony has had as crucial an influence on American history as any president, general, or inventor in this book. From a young age, Susan advocated for women's right to vote, which cost her friendships, business contacts, and even once got her arrested. She never gave up, though, working long hours until her final goal was realized.

Although she didn't live long enough to see the Nineteenth Amendment become law, the country was headed in that direction when she died in 1906.

But Susan B. Anthony was so much more than just America's first women's rights activist. She was a leading figure in the temperance movement, which was also briefly victorious when the Eighteenth Amendment was passed prohibiting alcohol and was outspoken in favor of labor, children's rights, and the rights of Blacks.

Susan B. Anthony was ahead of her time, although interestingly, the times almost caught up with her. Due to her efforts, Susan B. Anthony is America's premier activist heroine.

AN INHERITANCE OF ACTIVISM

Susan was born on February 15, 1820 in Adams, Massachusetts to Daniel and Lucy Anthony. The 1820s was a time of incredible change in the United States that directly affected the woman Susan would become.

Immigration from Scandinavia, Ireland, and the German-speaking kingdoms allowed the Northwest (what is now the Midwest) to be settled by pioneers, although more than a few Native American tribes had something to say about it.

The temperance movement was also gaining steam across the eastern states. This movement aimed to reduce alcohol consumption in the United States and was often aligned with religious groups.

Temperance activists believed that alcohol consumption was responsible for much of the nation's ills, including declining morals. Early feminists like Susan B. Anthony also made alliances with temperance groups because they believed that alcohol consumption led to domestic violence.

The 1820s was also a period of religious fervor, with new religious sects—such as the Mormons—regularly popping up across the land.

Sectionalism between the North and the South was becoming more apparent and abolitionist groups were organizing and disseminating their ideas to the public.

This was the world Susan B. Anthony was born into and, within her home, she was raised with conservative, yet progressive, values. The combination may seem strange today, but in the 1800s, it was quite common.

Daniel Anthony was a Quaker, but Lucy was a Methodist. The parents instilled Christian values and teachings into Susan and her six siblings, but they also taught their children about worldly activism.

Daniel was an outspoken abolitionist and temperance activist, which intensified after the family moved to Upstate New York. The Anthony farm served as a beacon of sorts, drawing notable American activists to it, including anti-slavery activist Frederick Douglass.

LONG BEFORE THE EQUAL RIGHTS AMENDMENT

By the early 1850s, Susan found herself in the middle of the burgeoning women's suffrage movement and the early feminist movement. Along with Elizabeth Cady Stanton, who was another notable early suffrage activist, Anthony wrote pamphlets and delivered speeches and lectures for a variety of different groups, including at several National Women's Rights Conventions.

But all the speeches and writings in the world would have been no good if the laws weren't ultimately changed. Not only did women not have the right to vote, they had very few rights in general and had little control of sizable finances. So, Anthony had to appeal to male lawmakers and revenue streams.

Susan experienced one of her first successes when the New York state legislature passed the Married Women's Property Act in 1848, which gave wives joint custody of their children and allowed them to separate their assets in marriage.

The Civil War slowed but didn't stop Anthony's activities. She took the time to focus some of her energies on other causes that she believed in and that were connected to the suffrage movement. Anthony helped organize for the temperance movement, believing that alcoholism contributed to domestic violence and a general environment where women and children were placed in danger.

Anthony was also an anti-slavery advocate and then an early pioneer for Black civil rights. She saw the Fourteenth Amendment, which recognized Black males as American citizens, as progress, but always pointed out that it denied Black women those same rights.

Anthony also advocated for organized labor and farmers, but by far her primary cause was women's rights, particularly the right to vote.

In 1866, the American Equal Rights Association (AERA) formed with the sole intent of pushing for women's suffrage. Anthony began publishing the radically named newspaper *The Revolution* in 1868 to disseminate AERA's news. AERA was immediately successful, but it also faced several challenges.

There were many men—even among Anthony's supporters—who wanted her to tone down her rhetoric. Her alliances with Black civil rights and labor groups were not always successful, either. Anthony found that many Black leaders wanted women to take a back seat to their movement and that labor groups were, for the most part, unwilling to support female labor unions and organizations.

Still, Susan B. Anthony fought on.

Anthony formed the National Women Suffrage Association (NWSA) in 1869 and later brought her movement overseas, speaking and organizing for women's rights in Europe.

But Susan B. Anthony was more than just an organizer or a speaker. Her ability to do those things certainly made her an important person in the history of women's rights in the United States. What made her a heroine in many people's eyes was her willingness to sacrifice and put her ideas into action. Susan B. Anthony's chance to do that came on election day 1872.

The NWSA began assuming a more proactive stance toward voting rights in the early 1870s, based primarily on the Fourteenth Amendment. To test their theory and to bring the issue of women's voting rights to the forefront, several suffragettes, including Susan B. Anthony, attempted to vote in the 1872 election. Susan was an activist who practiced what she preached and *"walked the walk."*

Anthony and her group were arrested by federal marshals for attempting to vote on November 18, 1872. Of the women who attempted to vote, only Anthony was arrested and faced jail time. It was clear that the government intended to make an example of her.

Despite the deprivations that she endured, Susan kept in high spirits during the months before her trial. She traveled the country on a speaking tour, raising her public profile, as well as that of the women's suffrage movement.

When Anthony went to trial in May 1873, it was clear that the odds were stacked against her. Susan knew that she wasn't going to get a fair trial, so she used the kangaroo court to craft one of her best-remembered speeches.

On the final day of the trail, much to the chagrin of the judge and other men in the courtroom, Anthony gave a speech where she stated that women could only get their rights if they were to *"take it; as I have taken mine, and mean to take it at every possible opportunity."*

Although many people throughout the world were impressed with Anthony's speech, the judge wasn't. After the jury found Anthony guilty, the judge sentenced her to a $100 fine, to which she replied, *"I shall never pay a dollar of your unjustly penalty."*

FIGHTING UNTIL THE END

Susan B. Anthony continued to be quite active in old age, organizing, speaking, and writing about the causes that mattered most to her. Although she never lived to see her dream of women's suffrage become a nationwide reality, several states had adopted women's suffrage before she died. With that said, the Nineteenth Amendment never would have been a reality without Anthony's efforts.

Even when things were bleak and it looked as if the women's suffrage movement was going nowhere, Anthony continued to fight, eventually gaining supporters, and bringing legitimacy to her movement. After decades of hard work, Susan B. Anthony transformed the women's suffrage movement from being on the political fringes into the mainstream.

Perhaps most importantly, though, was the fact that Susan B. Anthony inspired—and continues to inspire—millions of Americans who view her as an icon and a true American heroine.

DID YOU KNOW?

- Susan B. Anthony never married and never had children.

- As an example of how much the country changed during her lifetime and how the women's suffrage movement went from fringe to mainstream, she consistently ran into financial troubles in the mid-1850s, but celebrated her 80th birthday at the White House with President William McKinley.

- Anthony made connections within both major political parties, but she made more lasting connections and raised more money for the Republican Party. The Democrats of the era were divided into two primary factions: segregationists in the South and working-class immigrants in the North. The Republicans, on the other hand, saw themselves as upholding traditional America, with many believing that women were key to that ideology.

- Anthony was opposed to the Fifteenth Amendment, which gave Black males the right to vote, because it didn't guarantee women the right to vote.

- Susan died in her Rochester, New York home on March 13, 1906 at the age of 86.

AL CAPONE
THE HERO OF THE DRINKING CLASS

At the complete opposite end of the moral spectrum from Susan B. Anthony was Al Capone. Susan B. Anthony rose to fame and became an American heroine by advocating for women's rights, while being a paragon of virtue by abstaining from alcohol and other activities deemed immoral at the time.

On the other hand, Al Capone earned his name by robbing, extorting, and killing his way to the top of a criminal empire. Capone was known to be a philanderer, quick-tempered, and extremely violent, even in a world where violence was second-hand.

With all that said, Al Capone was considered by many — and still is by some — to be an American hero.

A large segment of the American population viewed Al Capone as a true success who wasn't afraid to thumb his nose at the system, if need be. Much like Jesse James decades earlier, Americans romanticized Al Capone, not only as a rag to riches story, but also as a sort of modern Robin Hood — Capone donated some of his money to Chicago charities.

Capone became known during the era of Prohibition for providing alcohol to the masses who, for the most part, didn't agree with the ban on booze. The average American citizen didn't have a problem with Capone's booze activities, and they reasoned that anyone whom he killed was probably another gangster anyway.

Eventually, Capone's reputation grew and became legendary. Despite his portrayal in television shows and movies as a cold-blooded, ruthless mafioso — or possibly because of that — Capone is the most recognized and perhaps, one may dare say, loved, American gangster.

American rappers often use and invoke either his last name or his more sinister-sounding moniker, Scarface, and tours of his homes and haunts in Chicago are among the city's most popular tourist attractions.

Al Capone may not be the type of hero Americans have always wanted, but he is certainly the type we've occasionally earned and accepted.

THE ORIGINAL SCARFACE

Alphonse Gabriel Capone was born on the hard streets of Brooklyn, New York in 1899. His parents were honest, working-class Italian immigrants who tried to instill good values and ethics in Al and his eight siblings. They were only partially successful.

The Capones weren't totally at fault, since times were tough in New York City at the time, with Italian, Jewish, Irish, German, and Polish street gangs fighting each other over turf and rackets.

Young Al fell in with a succession of different gangs, the most notable being the Five Points gang. While serving as an enforcer with the Five Points gang, Capone began making valuable connections in the New York City underworld. Often known as Big Al, Capone wasn't afraid to use his fists to settle arguments. The hulking Capone had an intimidating manner that got him far in the underworld, but it also created problems for him.

Al Capone liked to drink, he liked the ladies, he liked to brag, and he liked violence. He feared no one or anything, which nearly got him killed one night. Capone was working as a bouncer at a Coney Island club called the Harvard Inn.

The Harvard Inn was owned by a gangster named Frankie Yale, who became the teenage Capone's mentor in all things criminal. On a summer night in 1917, when Al was working the door at the club, gangster Frank Gallucio came in with his girlfriend and his sister. Capone was immediately attracted to Gallucio's sister.

Capone asked Gallucio's sister out and after she refused and told her brother, her brother suggested they leave. Capone's reputation was already well-known around town and, although Gallucio was no punk, he didn't want the hassle.

As the group was leaving, Capone supposedly told Gallucio's sister that she *"had a nice ass."* The 5'6" Gallucio then called out the 5'10", 200-plus pound Capone to a fight. Capone readily accepted, believing he'd smash the smaller foe, but Gallucio had other ideas, pulling out a knife and slashing the left side of Capone's face.

Capone was left with a scar and a nickname, which he usually tried to hide and sometimes told people he got in World War I, even though he never fought in the war. It could've turned into something much bigger, but Yale squashed the feud between the two gangsters.

Capone fumed about the assault for two years, but an offer that he couldn't refuse eventually took him far from New York.

THE OUTFIT

In 1919, mobster Johnny Torrio invited Capone to Chicago to help with his bootlegging operations, to work as an enforcer, and to better establish the Italian Cosa Nostra in that city. Prohibition had just begun, which presented major opportunities for gangsters and black marketeers. Chicago had unlimited potential: it was America's second-largest city, filled with immigrants from European countries with well-established drinking cultures — Germany, Poland, and Ireland.

Chicago's cultural composition may have presented some business opportunities, but it also presented a problem for the Cosa Nostra. The Mafia was challenged by other ethnic gangs in the city, especially the North Side Gang.

So, Big Al and Torrio began turning up the heat on the predominantly Irish gangsters, burning down their businesses and ambushing their associates. The Northsiders didn't sit idly by, ambushing both Capone and Torrio at different times. It was all too much for the elder Torrio, who turned over the reins of the Chicago Cosa Nostra, known as the Outfit, to Capone in 1925.

Capone then embarked on one of the most fascinating, exciting, and successful tenures as a crime boss in American history. Although Al had little formal education, he was an intelligent guy who knew how to read people. He could tell when people were lying, and he also knew that public opinion was important. As soon as he became the boss of the Outfit, he made sure that the palms of Chicago and Cicero (the town he lived in) politicians, cops, and union leaders were thoroughly greased. This allowed him to pretty much act with impunity in Cook County.

Next, he embarked on a program that made him a hero in many millions of people's eyes. Unlike gangsters before him, he wasn't afraid to give interviews to the press.

The affable Capone wore nice clothes and, although never explicitly denying he ran speakeasies, always claimed to be a legitimate businessman who was just *giving the people what they want."* And the people sure seemed to love Capone.

Capone opened a soup kitchen in Chicago at the corner of 9th and State Street that served more than 120,000 people during the Great Depression. He also helped older people with their rent and was even said to have given money to random homeless people on the streets. Because of those efforts, and the fact that Prohibition was unpopular, Capone was cheered wherever he went, including sold-out baseball games.

But let's be real, Al Capone was no saint. He made it to the top of the Chicago underworld at a young age by bootlegging, running brothels and casinos, and most importantly, using violence.

Once Al was in complete control of the Outfit, he continued his war against the North Side Gang, which culminated in the 1929 St. Valentine's Day Massacre. On that day, Outfit gunmen ambushed the Northsiders at one of their hideouts, killing seven.

It was one of the most brazen and bloody gangland massacres in American history up to that time and marked the beginning of the end for Al's phenomenal run.

Although Capone was never convicted, or even arrested, for having anything to do with the St. Valentine's Day Massacre, everyone knew he ordered it. Suddenly, the public began seeing Al Capone less as a lovable rebel and more as the cold-blooded gangster he was.

Al also had to face the relatively new Federal Bureau of Investigation (FBI). Capone may have had the Chicago and Cook County law enforcement agencies in his pocket, but the FBI officially made him their *"public enemy number one."* FBI director J. Edgar Hoover made it his mission to put Capone behind bars, but it wasn't easy.

By the late 1920s, the federal government was constantly investigating Capone, hoping to get him on anything. No one in Chicago was willing to testify against him and the few who agreed to ended up dead or missing, so the government decided to take another route. Instead of trying to get him on murder or another big crime, they'd go after him for several smaller crimes.

The government's first success came in 1929 when they arrested Capone for carrying a concealed weapon in Philadelphia. Since he had amassed a laundry list of enemies over his career as a gangster, Capone was very paranoid and always armed.

The feds knew this and decided to swoop in for the arrest. Al pled guilty and spent nine months in the notorious Eastern State Penitentiary in Philadelphia, but for Capone it was *"easy time,"* as his money and influence bought him protection and whatever else he wanted.

In the end, the feds finally put Capone away for tax evasion. Capone never reported his ill-gotten gains and never, in fact, used a bank. The idea of putting people in prison for tax evasion in 1931 was a very new thing. The federal income tax didn't become law until 1909 with the Sixteenth Amendment and prosecuting people for tax evasion was pretty rare. But they sure got Capone.

Al Capone was convicted of tax evasion in 1931 and sentenced to 11 years in prison. When he was released in 1939, Capone was a shell of a man suffering from the effects of long-term syphilis. Capone died in Florida on January 25, 1947 at the age of 48.

AL CAPONE, O.G.

Long before Mafia don John Gotti dazzled the American media with his larger-than-life personality, Robin Hood persona, and keen sense of style, earning himself the nickname Dapper Don, Al Capone played the role. He brought booze to the people of Chicago and for a time helped many working men escape the dreary reality of the Great Depression, either by getting drunk on his booze or by living vicariously through him.

And long before Al Pacino played a Cuban gangster called Scarface, and even before Capone's contemporary Charles Luciano became known as Scarface, Al Capone held the title, even if begrudgingly.

He may not have been a good example of morality, or even a

nice guy, but there is no denying that he played an important role in American history. There is also no denying that Al Capone is truly America's original gangster, who still inspires people around the world to live life on their terms.

DID YOU KNOW?

- After he died, Al's body was transported back to Chicago and buried between his parents in the Mount Carmel Cemetery in the western Chicago suburb of Hillside, Illinois. His gravesite has become a popular tourist attraction.

- Al married his wife Mae in 1918. The couple had one child, Albert, who was deaf in one ear.

- Two of Al's brothers, Ralph and Frank, worked with him in Chicago. Frank was shot and killed by the Chicago police during an election riot, while Ralph lived to the ripe old age of 80, dying in 1974.

- Al had another brother named James, who left New York after Al's face was slashed. Ironically, James went into law enforcement and became a federal agent with the Bureau of Indian Affairs. Al and James lost contact with each other after James left New York.

- When Capone was sent to prison for tax evasion, he was initially housed in the federal prison in Atlanta before being transferred to the notorious Alcatraz prison. It is believed that Capone was suffering from dementia, or a dementia type illness brought on by syphilis. Due to his reduced mental state, Capone had problems protecting himself from other inmates and was stabbed while at Alcatraz.

THE WRIGHT BROTHERS
FIRST IN FLIGHT

When we met Neil Armstrong earlier in this book, we noted how man has always looked to the skies. It is also true that man has always sought to be above our planet and fly with the birds.

The concept of flight has been the subject of numerous fictional stories, myths, and scientific experiments since the beginning of recorded history.

The Greek myth of Icarus tells of a bright young man who fashions wings that allow him to fly, but because of his arrogance, he gets too close to the sun and dies. Later in history, philosophers and scientists theorized that flight was possible. In the Middle Ages, Chinese scientists drew sketches of proposed flying machines, as did Leonardo da Vinci during the Renaissance.

Hot air balloons began taking people into the skies in the 1700s and the advances of the Industrial Revolution in the early 1800s meant that humankind was ready to take the next step—a motor propelled airplane.

In 1903, brothers Orville and Wilbur Wright successfully made that next leap forward after many trials and tribulations.

Incredibly, within a generation, their discovery was being used in full-scale warfare. In a mere 50 years, people were being shuttled around the world regularly in passenger airplanes.

The invention of the airplane has had such monumental repercussions on the world that it may be the greatest invention in history. For that reason, both of the Wright brothers stand — or should that be soar? — as two of America's greatest heroes.

IT ALL STARTED WITH BIKES

The Wright brothers were born in the American Midwest during a time of great change in the world. Wilbur was born in 1867 in Indiana and Orville was born in 1871 in Ohio.

Their father was a bishop in the United Brethren in Christ, moving the family a lot throughout the Midwest from church to church. The constant moves meant that the boys had few chances to make lasting friendships, but it also brought them closer together.

Neither of the Wright brothers impressed their grade school or high school teachers. Orville only completed three years of high school before he decided to start his own printing business. Of the two young Wrights, many thought Wilbur would be the one to make the most of his life, likely through athletics.

The young Wilbur was very athletic and quite good at most of the popular sports of the day. However, he was seriously injured in a hockey game when a puck hit him in the face, which ultimately ruined any chances he had at an athletic career and prevented him from attending college.

Wilbur became even closer to Orville after the injury and the two decided to make their way in the world together. Both brothers were self-taught engineers and scientists who loved to tinker with whatever mechanical devices they could find. But tinkering is no way to make a living, so they decided to open a bicycle repair shop in Dayton, Ohio in 1892.

At the time, the bicycle was a pretty new device. The earliest bicycles were the so-called penny-farthing design, which was a bike that had a front wheel that could be four feet tall.

The penny-farthing bikes weren't really practical, or safe, so when the standard design of bicycles hit the streets in the late 1880s, they quickly became popular. The new bikes were safe and easy to ride, giving the rider a practical vehicle for travel as well as for entertainment and as a past time.

Like all of our other hero scientists in this book, the Wright Brothers were entrepreneurs as well as scientists. They knew that the safety bike would take off, so they repaired and sold bikes. In 1896, the Wright Brothers began manufacturing a line of bikes, which netted them a nice sum of money.

Many men would've considered their lives a success and stopped right there, or possibly continued to build the bike business in Dayton. But the Wright boys were always looking ahead and to the skies. The profits they made from their bike business gave them the freedom to do what they wanted and is what made them American heroes.

LOOKING TO THE SKIES

As already mentioned, man has dreamed of flying with the birds for millennia. By the time the Wright Brothers officially began their quest to fly with the birds, they were not the only ones attempting to do so. They had some of the early theories to look at, such as the ideas of da Vinci, and other experiments that had been made on *"heavier than air"* flying machines.

The Wright Brothers continued to work at their bike business, and in their free time they worked countless hours on numerous designs for what they hoped would be the first mechanically powered, human-driven airplane.

English engineer Sir George Cayley (1773–1857) was the first person to scientifically consider heavier than air, fixed-wing flying machines (what we know today as an airplane), publishing his ideas in 1852. Although Cayley never built a working airplane, the Wright Brothers were influenced by his work.

As the two continued to work on their plane, they were faced with some stiff competition that included college-educated, world-renowned engineers Samuel Pierpont Langley and Octave Chanute. Both of these men had already built prototypes of airplanes but had failed to make them fly.

The Wright Brothers started constructing their plane with the body and wings; the motor was added later. They believed — and were proved right—that the body was the most important part of the craft. It had to be agile enough to glide through the air, yet it also had to be strong enough to carry a person and a motor.

When the Wright brothers arrived at the desolate, sandy dunes of the North Carolina coastline in December 1903, they had already tested motor-less versions of their flying machine, which we would call a glider. The design needed to be modified several times and it wasn't always pretty. The first glider attempt was a failure.

This upset the brothers so much that Orville wrote their sister a letter in which he stated that the two were considering quitting their venture and going back to Ohio.

The failure was compounded by the fact that their testing ground was located in desolate Kitty Hawk, North Carolina. Kitty Hawk is located near windswept dunes on a barrier island, which was great for the Wright Brothers experiments but not so good for their mental states.

Still, despite the loneliness of Kitty Hawk and the apparent failure of their design, the two brothers continued with their efforts. The glider crashed once more with Wilbur as pilot, but the brothers then felt confident enough in their knowledge and abilities that they could iron out the problems and fit the glider with an engine to make it the world's first airplane.

Designing the plane's engine also proved to be another barrier. Orville and Wilbur first attempted to get an automaker to specifically design an engine for their plane, arguing that it would prove to be a boon to whichever company got on board with the project. They were turned down by every company; even the usually outward-looking Henry Ford said that the project was doomed to fail!

The Wright Brothers overcame the engine problem by designing their own, along with a new type of propeller that they had to make specifically for their plane. With the engine and propeller created, the brothers then made another trip from Ohio to North Carolina.

Finally, after years of hard work, the Wright Brothers

achieved the dream of the ancients by flying with the birds on December 17, 1903, when Orville flew the plane 120 feet at 12 feet high.

HEROES OF CHANGE

The role that the Wright Brothers played in the formation of the modern world cannot be overstated. Consider the fact that they were born in the years after the American Civil War when railroads had just connected the United States and the first automobiles were being invented. By the time Orville died in 1948, telephones were common, freeways were spreading across America, and jet airplanes were being produced.

All of those great technological advances were either directly or indirectly related to the Wright Brothers' historic flight. By pushing the boundaries of perceived limits, the Wright Brothers opened up new avenues of innovation for other engineers and scientists. They showed that limits are meant to be pushed and many barriers should be broken.

The Wright Brothers proved that even the mild-mannered can be among the greatest heroes of American history.

DID YOU KNOW?

- Neither of the Wright Brothers married nor had children.

- The Wright Brothers had five other siblings (one died in infancy), but they were closest to their sister Katharine (1874–1929). She became the face of the Wright Brothers' business after their historic flight and accompanied them on trips around the U.S. and Europe.

- Wilbur Wright died in 1912 at the age of 45 of typhoid fever.

- As was common with major inventions of the era, the Wright Brothers had to fight others over their patent. Others claimed to have successfully flown planes earlier than them, but those flights were never properly documented.

- Before Orville died in 1948, he reflected on the airplane's recent use in World War II: *"I don't have any regrets about my part in the invention of the airplane, though no one could deplore more than I do the destruction it has caused. I feel about the airplane much the same as I do in regard to fire."*

ABRAHAM LINCOLN
HERO OF THE AMERICAN UNION

The Civil War was not only the costliest war in American history in terms of lives lost but also in the amount of physical destruction it left on the American landscape. Large swaths of the South were leveled by Union troops and the general cost to the American economy and infrastructure was immense.

Several causes led to the Civil War, including growing cultural differences between the North and South, disagreements over congressional representation and, of course, slavery. The issue of slavery was the underpinning of all the other problems, but the preservation of the American Union was the primary reason why most volunteers fought for the North and why Abraham Lincoln devoted all of his resources toward winning the war.

Lincoln's views on race are outdated by today's standards to say the least, and although he disagreed with slavery, it was an issue he would've put on the political back burner if need be. To Lincoln, preserving the American Union took precedence over everything.

And if you think about it, he was right.

The Southern states chose to leave the Union first, which meant that he was faced with a greater decision than any president before him. Let the Southern states leave peacefully and start their own country, or fight to keep them in the Union? Of course, Lincoln chose the latter, which wasn't an easy choice, but it proved to be the right one.

Abraham Lincoln preserved the Union and ended slavery, laying the groundwork for modern America in the process. He became a martyr for his vision, which instantly made him a hero, and as the decades went by, he became arguably the second-most popular president after George Washington.

NOT BORN WITH A SILVER SPOON

Most modern American presidents were born into privilege of one type or another. They have either been born with money, influence, connections, or a combination of all three. This is not to say that these presidents didn't endure any hardships, only that they were born with — or acquired at a young age — some advantages that most Americans don't have.

This was not the case with America's 16th president.

Abraham Lincoln was born on February 12, 1809 in a one-room cabin in rural Kentucky. Most of his early years were spent working on the family farm, which gave him little time for formal schooling. He did occasionally have tutors, though, and was able to educate himself quite nicely. Young Abraham's thoughts were always on his books and usually not on his farm work.

It was tough for Abraham to become acclimated and make friends, as his family moved from Kentucky to Indiana and then Illinois. Since the Lincolns were a farming family, and because Abraham was a strong young man, he was expected to do more than his share of the workload. But it was clear to all who knew him that young Abraham just wasn't cut out for farm work. He did what he had to, but his heart was never in the work.

When Abraham was 23, he ventured out on his own and tried his hand at being a merchant. Although his business eventually failed, it gave him the chance to meet different people, make connections, and see the country, as he bought and sold products in different parts of the eastern U.S.

Lincoln was never the type of person who would let a minor setback get him down. He briefly served in the Illinois state militia during the Black Hawk War (1832), which gave him even more important connections and the type of cache that a politician needed at that time. But by the late 1830s, he finally settled on a career in law.

At that time, most lawyers were self-educated, having only to pass the bar exam in their state to practice law. Lincoln passed the Illinois bar exam in 1836 and went on to build a successful law practice. He became particularly known for his oratory and debate skills, with his large frame helping add to his persuasiveness.

Lincoln had settled into his own by 1840, when he married Mary Todd and was at the top of his professional and personal life. The Lincolns' had four sons and, by all accounts, spoiled their children. Yet as good as life may have seemed for Lincoln, tragedy was never far.

The Lincolns' second oldest son, Eddie, died in 1850 of tuberculosis and their third son, Willie, died in the White House in 1862 of a fever. It seemed as if there was always some type impediment in Abraham Lincoln's life that would've stopped many people, but he always kept moving forward.

As Abraham established his successful law practice and family in the 1840s, he was working his way through the Illinois state political system.

DEBATING HIS WAY TO THE TOP

For Lincoln, and many of those who knew him, politics seemed like a logical step. He had made many important connections by the 1830s and had the requisite speaking and debating skills needed for a political career. His first foray into politics came when he ran for a seat in the Illinois state assembly in 1832 as a member of the Whig Party. Although he lost in a landslide, he regathered and came back to win the seat in a landslide in 1834.

Working as a lawyer and representative, Lincoln increased his reach and won a U.S. House seat in 1846. After serving only one term, Lincoln went back to being a full-time lawyer, but Illinois and the nation hadn't heard the last of the frontiersman lawyer.

Although Lincoln was not in the public eye for the first few years of the 1850s, he maintained his political connections in the decaying Whig Party. The issues of slavery and immigration were the two hottest topics in the 1850s and the Democrat Party had clear stances on both.

Southern Democrats favored slavery and didn't have much of a stance on immigration, since few immigrants were migrating to the South. Northern Democrats courted the Irish and German votes while maintaining a neutral stance on slavery and a sometimes hostile stance toward Northern Blacks.

The Whigs were all over the place on both of those issues. Eventually, anti-slavery Whigs aligned with anti-slavery Democrats and the members of the anti-immigrant American Party to form the Republican Party. Lincoln reinvented himself as an anti-slavery Republican, without displaying too much anti-immigrant rhetoric.

Lincoln became a national figure when he was nominated to be the Illinois Republican Party's U.S. Senate candidate. He immediately made an impact when he delivered the now-famous *"House Divided Speech,"* where he stated, *"A house divided against itself cannot stand. I believe this government cannot endure permanently half slave and half free."*

His opponent was Democrat Stephen Douglas. The two men locked horns in seven public debates that became known as the Lincoln–Douglas Debates. Both men were impressive, but Lincoln was defeated, as much by the system as Douglas.

At that time, U.S. senators were chosen by their state assemblies, and although more Illinoisans voted for Republicans in that election, the Democrats won more seats, giving the senate seat to Douglas.

But Lincoln became the most recognized Republican nationally, which earned him the Republican Party's presidential nomination in 1860.

KEEPING THE COUNTRY TOGETHER

Lincoln won the presidency in 1860 with plenty of electoral votes to spare but only 39% of the popular vote. The Southern slave states voted overwhelmingly for Democrat John Breckinridge, while the border states voted for Constitutionalist John Bell. Stephen Douglas also ran and took Missouri.

Lincoln's election pushed the South over the edge into open rebellion and secession.

Once the Civil War began, things became even more complicated for Lincoln. Public opinion was clearly on his side at first, but as General Lee scored some victories, people began doubting Lincoln's decision-making abilities. Many also weren't happy with Lincoln suspending *habeas corpus*.

The Sioux Uprising in Minnesota during the summer of 1862 also tested Lincoln's abilities to wage war.

By late 1862, it was clear to Lincoln that he had to make some major moves on and off the battlefield. He issued the *Emancipation Proclamation* on September 22, 1862, freeing all slaves in the Confederate states. He then promoted Ulysses S. Grant to be the top commander of the Union Army.

The moves paid off, as Lincoln was reelected in 1864 and the Union won the war in 1865.

The devastation of the Civil War deeply hurt Lincoln. He hated to see the South ripped up and was saddened to see so many lives lost on the battlefield. When Lincoln gave the famed Gettysburg Address on November 19, 1863, he stated that he hoped America would be united again: *"These dead shall not have died in vain – that this nation, under God, shall have a new birth of freedom."*

After the war ended, all accounts show that Lincoln intended to go easy on the former Confederate states, with a more reconciliatory policy. In a tragic and ironic twist, he was gunned down by Confederate sympathizer John Wilkes Booth on April 14, 1865 and died the next day.

The hardline Radical Republicans then took power and punished the South for its rebellion.

THE SPIRIT OF THE UNION

Today, Abraham Lincoln is remembered as the man who ended slavery, the president who led the country during the Civil War, and the father of the Republican Party.

Although he was responsible for all those things to a certain extent, he should best be remembered as the man who preserved the American Union. The United States faced its first true crisis in the years leading up to, and then during, the Civil War, which very easily could have divided the country for good.

The greatest fight of Lincoln's life was to keep the United States united. The reality is that he only declared war after the South seceded and very reluctantly freed the slaves, which wasn't due to weakness or indecision, but because he knew that the American Union was threatened.

The American Union probably wouldn't have survived if other men were leading it during that tumultuous period.

But Abraham Lincoln made preserving the Union his number one priority, and for that reason, he is considered the first president of America's second era and, arguably, the greatest president of all time.

DID YOU KNOW?

- At 6′4″, Lincoln was by far the tallest of American presidents. Due to Lincoln's height and his extra-long limbs, especially his hands, some scientists believe he suffered from Marfan syndrome.

- Lincoln was a wrestler in his teens and early twenties in New Salem, Illinois. Although the matches he wrestled were far less organized, the National Wrestling Hall of Fame inducted him into its ranks in 1992.

- One of Lincoln's best-known nicknames is the Great Emancipator, although it didn't become popular until after his death.

- Lincoln had two vice presidents serve under him: Hannibal Hamlin from Maine for his first term and Andrew Johnson from Tennessee for his second term.

- Abraham suffered from health problems all his life. He suffered from bouts of smallpox and malaria when he was young and modern scholars also think he fought depression for much of his life.

JIM THORPE
FROM INDIAN TERRITORY
TO THE OLYMPICS

Long before Bo Jackson and Deion Sanders made headlines for being professional two-sport athletes, Jim Thorpe had successfully blazed those trails. Taking American sports by storm in the 1910s and '20s, Jim Thorpe became a household name, first as a gold medalist Olympian and then as a professional baseball, football, and basketball player.

Along with Babe Ruth, Thorpe became one of America's first true sports heroes and was universally loved and respected, which was incredible considering his background.

Jim Thorpe was born in 1887 in what was known at the time as Indian Territory and what is today the state of Oklahoma. Both of his parents were of mixed European and American Indian ancestry and Jim was raised as a Native American.

There was no denying that Thorpe was an American Indian. Standing at 6'1", Thorpe's Sac and Fox tribal heritage was flowing strongly through his veins — based on his appearance alone one would've thought he was full-blooded American Indian.

Thorpe's ethnic background makes his story all that more

interesting and important.

When Thorpe was becoming a multi-sport star, the idea of cowboys versus Indians was still very real in many people's minds. Many survivors of the Indian Wars were still alive, and many American Indians weren't given full citizenship until 1924.

Despite the history and attitudes that were associated with his background, Jim Thorpe became an American icon and a true hero to millions of people.

BRIGHT PATH

Jim Thorpe began his life in 1887 in the Indian Territory with his feet in two worlds. His father, Hiram, was half White and half Sac and Fox Indian, while his mother, Charlotte, was half White and half Potawatomi Indian. His parents instilled him with both American/Western values and those of his Native ancestors.

Jim was baptized in the Roman Catholic Church and was a practicing Catholic for his entire life, but he also maintained close roots to his indigenous ancestry. He was given a Sac and Fox name at birth that roughly translates to Bright Path, which was surely true of his later professional sports career.

But first he had to make it through childhood.

Jim's twin brother died when he was just nine and then his mother died two years later. Thorpe was close to both, so the quick succession of deaths deeply affected the young boy, who took to rebelling against his father and his teachers. He ran away from home and was eventually sent to the famed

Carlisle Indian Industrial School in Carlisle, Pennsylvania.

The Carlisle School was the first federally funded off-reservation school and was created to assimilate American Indians into mainstream American culture. Although the goal of the Carlisle School is criticized today by some, its tactics were far more humane than many of the notorious reservation schools. Carlisle offered a curriculum similar to most other public schools of the period and offered extracurricular activities, including sports.

It was at Carlisle where Jim Thorpe was first introduced to organized sports by legendary football coach Glenn *"Pop"* Warner.

In case you don't already know, Pop Warner is the man who singlehandedly made American football/gridiron football one of the three most popular team sports north of the Rio Grande. Warner successfully coached several college football teams, and in between coaching big-name schools such as Iowa State, Georgia, and Stanford, he coached at the Carlisle School.

Warner took the Carlisle Indians football team, as they were called, against some of the top college programs in America at the time, winning their fair share of games. Carlisle was successful due to Warner's coaching and the will and tenacity of the players, despite usually being outsized by the other schools.

Thorpe first met Warner when he ran track for him on the track team in 1907. Thorpe was by far the best athlete on the team, so when Thorpe expressed his desire to play football, Warner was initially hesitant.

It wasn't that Warner didn't think Thorpe could play — quite the opposite actually — but more so that he thought he could get injured, which would cost Warner his best runner. Warner decided to let him play and the rest was history.

Thorpe played several positions on the football team, as well as being the school's star baseball player, lacrosse player, and track star. He shattered records, ran over future President Dwight Eisenhower when Carlisle played Army, and was a first-team All-American in 1911 and 1912, becoming the first American Indian to hold that honor.

It was clear to everyone who watched Thorpe play that he had a future in the burgeoning field of professional American sports; it was just a matter of what sport he wanted to play.

A TRUE SPORTS STAR

Before Thorpe would make a career in professional sports, he competed in the 1912 Summer Olympics in Stockholm, Sweden. Thorpe was joined on the American team by future General George Patton, but Thorpe was the hero of the games.

Jim competed in the grueling pentathlon and decathlon events, easily winning both. Due to his Olympic success, Thorpe became an instant celebrity and was given a ticker-tape parade in New York, but the recognition also brought more scrutiny on his life. After it was revealed that Jim played some semi-pro baseball before the Olympics, the Olympic committee stripped him of his medals.

Being stripped of the medals may have been a setback for many, but Thorpe used the event to his advantage. He signed with the New York baseball Giants in 1913 and played professional baseball at the Major League level until 1919. Although he never became the star of the baseball diamond that Babe Ruth was, Thorpe had a relatively successful career.

But it would be on the football gridiron where Jim Thorpe became a legend.

From 1920 to 1928, Thorpe played 52 games in the professional National Football League for five different teams: the Cleveland Indians, the Rock Island Independents, the New York football Giants, the Canton Bulldogs, and the Chicago Cardinals.

Thorpe also played for a couple of so-called barnstorming teams — the Tampa Cardinals and the Oorang Indians — which were teams that traveled the country playing any team available, professional or college.

Thorpe also coached many of the teams on which he played.

During the 1920s, the only athlete better known in America was Babe Ruth, but Jim Thorpe wasn't far behind. Unlike Ruth, Thorpe turned his fame into a brief but lucrative film career in the 1930s.

Unfortunately, once the limelight faded from Jim Thorpe's life, so too did his health. After he retired from professional sports he descended into a decades-long battle with alcoholism, which contributed to his death from a heart attack in 1953 at the age of 65.

AN AUTHENTIC AMERICAN HERO

There were no better all-round athletes in the early 1900s than Jim Thorpe, and few have been able to come close since. Like his contemporary Babe Ruth, Thorpe accomplished his achievements through a combination of raw talent and hard work; he didn't have the luxury of expensive trainers, modern equipment, or performance-enhancing drugs.

Jim Thorpe's athletic feats were certainly enough to make him a hero, but when one considers the period in which he was alive, they are all that much more incredible. Thorpe became a household name, and a genuine American hero, at a time when American Indians still hadn't yet received full citizenship status in the United States and there were still lingering resentments over the Indian Wars.

Perhaps because he was raised with one foot in mainstream American culture and another in American Indian culture, Jim Thorpe was able to rise above those differences and antagonisms and become a beloved American icon.

Because of his accomplishments on the field and his attitude in everyday life, Jim Thorpe will always be America's first gridiron hero.

DID YOU KNOW?

- Although Thorpe is sometimes compared to Babe Ruth because they were the two premier American athletes of the era, the men had vastly different personalities. Ruth was known to love the limelight and the press, while Thorpe was more reserved and a bit introverted.

- Most Jim Thorpe sports trading cards are worth some money, but if you have his 1933 Goudey Sport Kings card, it's worth a cool $1,500!

- Thorpe was married three times and had eight children.

- His first professional football contract was with the Canton Bulldogs in 1915 for $250. It may not seem like much, but that was a lot of cash at the time. The team justified the higher than average salary because Thorpe was already a household name from the Olympics and baseball, so they believed, correctly so, that he would increase ticket sales.

- Thorpe was inducted into the inaugural class of the Pro Football Hall of Fame in 1963 and continues to be thought of as one of the best football players of all time. The college football award for the best defensive back is called the Jim Thorpe Award.

HENRY FORD
MAKING AMERICA SMALLER

Here in the United States, we all love our cars. The United States is fourth in the world per capita for automobile ownership, only behind San Marino, Monaco, and New Zealand. Europeans often scoff at the American love of automobiles, especially the big trucks and SUVs that you won't find in most other countries. The reality is that a car is almost indispensable in the U.S.

As you know, the U.S. is a big country, and Americans tend to move a lot for jobs and other opportunities, so having a car is convenient to visit far off friends and family. Many Americans also live a distance from their jobs and not near accessible public transportation. Not to mention that public transportation in the U.S. is often notoriously unreliable.

So, most Americans need to have a car, but thankfully cars are quite affordable in the U.S.

We all have Henry Ford to thank for the automobile's *afford*ability — yes, pun intended!

Many people often mistakenly think that Henry Ford invented the automobile. Although he was one of the early pioneers of the technology, that honor is usually given to Karl Benz.

What Henry Ford did do, though, was to take the idea of the car and combine it with the idea of the modern assembly line, which made it easier and cheaper for his factory to make the quintessentially American Model T Ford.

Once the assembly lines began churning out Model Ts in 1908, they were affordable for most working Americans, which drastically changed this country and the world.

The automobile became not so much about status of wealth, but more so about hard work, and that a person had *earned* the right to own a car. The mass production and affordability of the automobile also meant that as vast as the United States was, it suddenly became much smaller.

Americans could take a trip in a matter of hours that only ten years prior may have taken days. The emergence of the automobile gave people more opportunities for work and business as well. By 1913, the federal government began construction on the Lincoln Highway, which was the first highway to traverse the U.S. from the east coast to the west coast.

By the time Henry Ford died in 1947, freeways were beginning to sprawl across the country and the automobile had become America's favorite mode of transportation. Henry Ford changed the way life was lived in America and most people would probably say it has been for the better.

THE PRIDE OF DEARBORN

Henry Ford was born in a rural area outside Detroit, Michigan in 1863 and lived most of his life in the area, namely the town of Dearborn. Young Henry's parents placed him in grade school for a traditional education, but he didn't do particularly well in the regimented environment.

Although he was an enthusiastic kid, he was a poor speller and reader, which often translated into poor grades.

There is a strong possibility that Ford had dyslexia but was undiagnosed.

The story could've ended there, with young Henry Ford going on to become a farmer or a factory worker, but instead, he persisted to become one of America's greatest heroes.

Young Henry may have performed poorly in formal schooling, but he proved to be a whiz when it came to practical science and engineering. Ford taught himself how to fix small engines and watches. In no time, his parents were supporting his professional endeavors by bringing him customers for his burgeoning watch repair business.

Henry probably could've made a modest living fixing watches and small engines around his parents' home in Dearborn, but he was a visionary, just like the other scientist heroes we've met in this book. Also, like Edison, Bell, and the Wright Brothers, Ford was an ambitious man.

The young mechanic landed a job as an engineer's apprentice in Detroit at the age of 16 but was fired after a few months.

As with his other setbacks, Ford used the job loss as a learning experience, eventually landing an even better position with the Edison Illuminating Company of Detroit in 1891.

INSPIRED BY GREATNESS

The Edison Illuminating Company was owned by none other than *the* Thomas Edison. Ford was given great latitude in the company to experiment and design early automobiles, which impressed Edison so much that he met with Ford in 1896.

The meeting had a profound impact on Henry Ford's life.

Ford had grown up idolizing the older Edison, so when the two men met in a Brooklyn Hotel in 1896, it inspired Ford and helped shape the trajectory of his career. Using Edison as a template as a successful scientist and businessman, Ford continued to develop new cars and left Edison's company to go into business for himself.

Ford, along with several partners, formed the Detroit Automobile Company in 1899. Ford's first company did not last long, though, because in 1901 he had lost $86,000 on a line of trucks that the company built, which effectively put the company out of business.

But as was common with all of our American heroes, failure was never a permanent state for Henry Ford. Instead, it was seen as a potential learning opportunity. As Ford once so succinctly put it, *"Failure is simply the opportunity to begin again, this time more intelligently."*

So, Henry formed the Henry Ford Motor Company in 1901, but left after only one year. That company would then become Cadillac Automobile Company.

Henry was finally able to use the knowledge, connections, and money he had acquired over his young career to build a company that truly fit his vision. In 1903, with the help of

John and Horace Dodge—yes, they are the guys who the Dodge automobile was named after—and other investors, Ford was able to open the Ford Motor Company to build the visionary Model T line.

The Model T entered the market in 1908 and decreased in price over the years.

From 1908 to 1927, more than 15 million Model Ts were made and during the peak of its popularity in the 1920s more than 10,000 were produced a day, outproducing all of Ford's competition combined!

The success of the Model T profoundly changed America, and the world, and made Henry Ford one of the most wealthy and influential people in America at the time. The success of his car and company gave him a high media profile, revealing how controversial and complex he could be.

Ford fought union influence in his factories wherever and whenever he could, but he paid his workers much higher wages than other, similar companies did, which raised the overall wages throughout much of the industry. Henry was also one of the first manufacturers to mandate a five-day workweek for his workers.

His political and racial views weren't out of the norm for the period; he believed that Whites should be in complete control, but he was also the largest employer of Black workers in Detroit throughout the 1920s.

Ford was considered a peace activist in his time, opposing American involvement in World War I, but he was also very anti-Semitic, using his newspaper *The Dearborn Independent* to forward many of his political and racial views. He also continued to do business with Nazi Germany right up until America's entry into World War II.

Henry was also a champion of international business and, one could say, an early globalist, yet he always placed Americans and the United States first in all of his visionary ideas.

A TRUE WORKING MAN'S HERO

Throughout history, many different figures have claimed to be advocates or fighters of the working-class: Karl Marx, Friedrich Engels, and countless other communist and socialist philosophers, luminaries, and revolutionaries come to mind. The reality is that extraordinarily little of what those people did have helped better the lives of blue-collar workers in any tangible way.

But there is no doubt that Henry Ford drastically improved the lives of most Americans when he rolled the first Model Ts off the production line in 1908. With the introduction of the Model T, many Americans could afford to own a car and to experience all the opportunities and enjoyment that comes with it.

It was no coincidence that the height of the Model T's popularity came during the 1920s, which was one of the periods of America's greatest material and cultural prosperity. You could easily argue that the Roaring '20s rode through the nation on the seat of a Model T, thanks to Henry Ford.

The Model T also made this country a bit smaller and brought everyone a little closer, which was surely a commendable thing.

DID YOU KNOW?

- Ford died on April 7, 1947 at his home in Dearborn, Michigan of a brain hemorrhage. He suffered from several strokes and heart attacks and probably also had dementia.

- Besides working as an engineer, inventor, scientist, and businessman, Ford worked in a sawmill and farmed for a brief period.

- Ford married his wife Clara in 1888. They had one child together, son Edsel, who was born in 1893. The failed Edsel car that was manufactured from 1957 to 1960 was named for Edsel Ford, who had died in 1943.

- The Model A was a successful follow up to the Model T, but as Ford's health declined, so too did the prospects of the company, beginning in the late 1930s.

- In his younger years, Ford was an avid car racer. In 1909, he won a cross country race in a modified Model T and also competed in numerous other races as a racer, builder, and team owner.

SEPTEMBER 11 FIRST RESPONDERS
RISKING EVERYTHING

For the most part, Americans have been blessed to live in a country that has been relatively free of war and upheaval. The British briefly invaded the United States during the War of 1812, and although the American Civil War did devastate this country, it was the only major war fought on American soil.

The United States has also avoided major political upheavals and political violence. Only four American presidents have been assassinated, none since 1963, there has never been a political coup and — outside of eruptions associated with the Vietnam War and the Civil Rights Movement in the 1960s — political violence has never threatened to collapse the system.

Compared to most other countries, even developed countries in Europe and Asia, the United States has been quite stable throughout its history, which made the events of September 11, 2001 so psychologically shocking for most Americans.

On that day, Islamic terrorists flew planes into the World Trade Center towers in New York City and the Pentagon in Washington, D.C. A final plane crashed in rural Pennsylvania after the passengers attacked the hijackers, more than likely preventing a third attack.

Nearly 3,000 people lost their lives in the attacks and more than $10 billion in damage was done, but as mentioned, the true damage was psychological. Americans were confused and perplexed by how and why people would do such a thing.

As Americans struggled to come to terms with the violence that had gripped the nation, a class of heroes stepped up to save countless lives, often sacrificing theirs in the process.

The first responders selflessly ran into the collapsing World Trade Center towers and the Pentagon to save as many people as they could. In doing so, they became some of the greatest American heroes in recent memory. The 9/11 first responders showed that, despite all our differences, Americans can come together in times of tragedy, and ultimately, come out stronger.

The September 11 first responders showed the terrorists that it would take more than a few terrorist attacks to take the country down.

THAT FATEFUL DAY

For those of us old enough to remember, September 11, 2001 began just as any early fall day. It was a warm, sunny morning in New York City, but not long after the workday began, at 8:46 EST, American Airlines Flight 11 crashed into the North Tower of the World Trade Center. No one knew what had happened. Sure, many thought it was a terrorist attack, but the idea that a malfunction on the plane had caused the crash was just as plausible.

Since it wasn't immediately known what caused the crash, orderly evacuation of part of the North Tower began. Officers from the New York City Police Department and the Port Authority, along with firefighters from the New York City Fire Department and emergency medical technicians, were all dispatched to the scene.

As the first responders were setting up stations around the World Trade Center, United Airlines Flight 175 hit the South Tower.

Everyone knew at that point it was some type of attack.

The firefighters led the charge, running into both buildings to pull as many people out as possible. For a time, it looked like they were going to get most of the people out.

The scene was chaotic. People were rushing for the stairs, fire alarms were going off, and the smell of burning metal and plastic permeated the air. To make matters worse, the firefighters were having a difficult time communicating through their radios, which made the next series of events truly devastating.

THE TOWERS COLLAPSE

Fire Marshal Ronald Bucca and Battalion Chief Orio Palmer were horrified to see people choosing to jump to their deaths from their office windows rather than be incinerated by the fire. The two men were marathon runners and perhaps the fittest in the fire department. So, without saying a word, they sprinted into the South Tower to rescue as many people from the inferno as possible.

It is believed that Bucca and Palmer got as far as the 78th floor before it all came crashing down.

America watched in horror as the South Tower collapsed at 9:59 am. It was at that point when the casualty count of the emergency workers began to escalate, but so too did their heroism.

Among the hundreds of people buried beneath the rubble of the South Tower was Fire Department Chief Peter Ganci Jr. Ganci was injured but still alive. He was somehow able to miraculously dig himself out of the rubble and return to the department's command post outside the North Tower.

He could've reported to the hospital, or even gone home, but Ganci instead met with Fire Department Commissioner William Feehan to strategize the plan to get people out of the North Tower.

There was virtually no communication with anyone inside the North Tower and they knew that it was only a matter of time before it too collapsed. However, they couldn't leave any of their people behind if there was still something they could do.

And the command post outside the North Tower desperately needed reinforcements.

When the South Tower collapsed, it launched a wave of deadly debris that had the effect of shrapnel, killing many people trying to escape the North Tower, and wiping out the fire department command post.

Among the firefighters killed at the command post was department chaplain Mychal Judge. Judge responded immediately after the first attack and was asked by Mayor Rudolf Giuliani to pray for the victims, which he did, but he also went into action.

Still, the firefighters, along with the police and EMTs, kept working until the North Tower collapsed at 10:28 am.

After the towers collapsed, only 23 people, including 15 first responders, were pulled from the rubble. It took weeks for the smoke from the attacks to clear, but when it did, the effects were devastating.

Among the rescue workers, the firefighters were hit the worst, losing 343 altogether. Seventy-five of New York's firehouses lost at least one member that day.

The Port Authority was next in the number of rescue workers killed, with 37 dead, including Superintendent Ferdinand Morrone and Chief James Romito. Both were assisting firefighters in the North Tower when it collapsed.

The New York City Police Department had 23 of their officers killed and eight EMTs who worked with private companies died on 9/11 trying to rescue people.

TRUE HEROES IN PERSPECTIVE

As much as the 9/11 attacks hurt and confused most Americans and shook our sense of security, the brave actions of the first responders gave all Americans something good and positive to rally behind.

No one could deny that those brave men and women who risked everything that day to save their fellow New Yorkers were heroes and were worthy of everyone's praise. But a big part of the story is that very few of the first responders tried to cash in on their experiences.

They were quite humble. Most just said they were doing their job, and many appeared genuinely hurt that they couldn't do more.

But what more could they have done? What would you or I have done?

Those are both legitimate questions. The answers prove the hero status of all the 9/11 responders.

There were little more the responders could have done, especially when you consider that the New York City Fire Department essentially lost all of its leadership that day. Firefighters like Ganci and Feehan, and police officers such as Morrone and Romito, could have played it safe from a distance and just sent other people into the inferno.

After all, many were close to receiving their pensions. But they risked it all, proving that there was no more they could do.

The answer to the second question is a little more complex and hypothetical. We all like to think that, in an emergency, we'll do the right thing. The reality is there's about a 50% chance that you would choose to save your skin (flight rather than fight).

There is nothing wrong with that; it's an evolutionary trait. But it's what makes the 9/11 first responders among the greatest of all-American heroes.

DID YOU KNOW?

- Although the number of deaths of first responders was high on September 11, 2001, many times that number may have died due to illnesses related to the attacks in subsequent years. More than 4,000 cases of cancer in the first responders have been linked to being at Ground Zero.

- First responders were equally as brave and heroic after the attack on the Pentagon, but none died in the rescue operations. The reason for the lower casualty count at the Pentagon in general, and specifically among first responders, is due to the firm structure and lower height of the Pentagon.

- It was reported that rescue dogs became depressed during the recovery operations at Ground Zero because they rarely found survivors. Their handlers would sometimes pose as survivors to raise their spirits.

- The James Zadroga 9/11 Health and Compensation Act of 2010 is a law that provides financial aid to 9/11 first responders whose health has been affected by the attacks. The law is named for NYPD officer James Zadroga, who died years after the attacks from respiratory disease.

- 27-year-old Keith Roma was the lone member of the New York City Fire Patrol to die in the 9/11 attacks.

THOMAS JEFFERSON
AMERICA'S PHILOSOPHER PRESIDENT

When it comes to America's presidents, the reality is that the greatest ones were very practical men. Let's take the two presidential heroes we've discussed so far: George Washington and Abraham Lincoln. By all accounts, both Washington and Lincoln were bright men, but they weren't what you would consider academics or even intellectuals.

They were for the most part—like most American presidents—practical men. After all, Americans are practical people, so they have historically tended to favor more plain-spoken leaders who at least appear down to earth.

Thomas Jefferson is one of the few exceptions to this rule. Without a doubt, he was the first and, arguably, the greatest intellectual or philosopher president.

Like many of the other Founding Fathers of the United States, Jefferson was born into privilege, but he didn't abuse that birthright. Instead, he built upon it throughout his life. By all accounts, he was a genius. Like his slightly older contemporary, Benjamin Franklin, he was also a Renaissance man.

Jefferson was the primary author of the Declaration of Independence, the nation's third president, and more than any of the early presidents, a true visionary. He saw a future where the entire country spanned the continent and where freedom-loving farmers and ranchers would till the soil and produce generations of farmer-philosophers.

Of course, Jefferson had his flaws, and some of his philosophies were not very practical, but his influence on America is immeasurable. If George Washington is the physical father of the United States, Thomas Jefferson is the nation's intellectual and spiritual father.

Thomas Jefferson may never have led armies into battle, but he proved that you can win a war with ideas.

A THIRST FOR KNOWLEDGE

Thomas Jefferson was a man who enjoyed learning, which began not long after he was born in Virginia in 1743 and continued until he died in 1826. Born into a wealthy planter family, young Thomas had the advantage of plenty of books and tutors, but unlike many of his contemporaries, he also received a formal education.

He was admitted to the College of William & Mary at the age of 16 and, by that time, he was already quite academically skilled. Jefferson could already speak and write French and Greek as well as Latin.

By his mid-20s, Jefferson was evolving into a regular Renaissance man. Besides his linguistic and writing skills, he was adept with several musical instruments and knew about nature and biology. Jefferson would later apply many of his ideas about biology to his plantation in Virginia, where he grew crops and raised livestock.

Farming was only a pastime for Jefferson, as he would make his true mark on the world as a philosopher and statesman; but first, he had to work his way up through the legal and political world.

Jefferson began his political career in the Virginia House of Burgesses. The House of Burgesses was the elected assembly for the colony of Virginia. Any native of Virginia who hoped to do anything politically either had to win a seat in the House of Burgesses or be deeply connected to those who had seats.

Jefferson served in the House of Burgesses from 1769 until 1775, just as events were transpiring that led to the American Revolution. Jefferson was critical of the British and their heavy-handed policies toward the American colonies, such as the Intolerable Acts, and by 1775, he was a full-blown Patriot.

The year 1775 was when the American Revolution began, and it was also the year that Jefferson was elected as a delegate from Virginia to the Continental Congress.

Jefferson would also serve as Governor of Virginia in the second half of the war (1779–1781), helping keep stability in the colony when British General Cromwell came storming through. However, it was his ideas that were most important to the American war effort.

THE DECLARATION OF INDEPENDENCE

Next to the United States Constitution, the Declaration of Independence is the most important legal document in American history and is what made Thomas Jefferson a bona fide American hero.

Jefferson was deeply influenced by the writings of Enlightenment philosophers such as John Locke, Thomas Hobbes, Montesquieu, and Jean-Jacques Rosseau. They argued that man had certain natural, *inalienable* rights, which meant that—no matter how despotic a leader may be—each man was still born free and should die free.

The leaders of the revolution chose Jefferson to draft the Declaration based on his intelligence and eloquence.

Over two weeks in June and July 1776, Jefferson wrote and rewrote the Declaration with the advisement of John Adams. Of course, the Declaration is best known for the second line, *"We hold these truths to be self-evident, that all men are created equal, that they are endowed by their Creator with certain unalienable Rights, that among these are Life, Liberty and the pursuit of Happiness."*

More importantly, the Declaration established why Americans broke free from Britain and documented some of Jefferson's vision for America.

After the war was over and America gained its freedom, Jefferson was able to do even more to forward his American vision when he became president.

JEFFERSON'S VISION OF AMERICA

Jefferson was elected the third President of the United States of America in 1800 amid growing political polarization in the country. The non-partisan honeymoon of Washington's presidency ended with the formation of the first political party system in America: The Federalist Party and the Democratic–Republican Party.

Although both parties were comprised of some of the original founding fathers, by Washington's second term, it became clear that there were two hugely different views of America's future.

Alexander Hamilton and second President John Adams believed that America should build an industrial base, give more power to the central government, enforce strong trade tariffs, and rebuild friendly relations with the British. This faction eventually became the Federalist Party, which was strong in the northeastern states.

On the other hand, Thomas Jefferson believed that America's future would be shaped by farmers, plantation owners, and ranchers and that low tariffs and a decentralized government were the best policies. This faction formed the Democratic–Republican Party, which was more commonly known as the Democrats. The Democrats were popular in the South and the new states and territories in the west.

Jefferson won the election and reelection, and the Democratic–Republicans became the dominant political party, largely because they supported increasing enfranchisement.

Jefferson thought that the only way that his vision of yeoman farmers spanning out across American could be achieved was if as many as possible took part in the government. For that to happen, as many as possible had to have the ability to vote.

Before Jefferson, only White male property owners could vote. Although Jefferson never supported Black males or women of any race voting, he led the charge to eliminate property requirements on voting. The effect was a dramatic increase in voter turnout and overall participation in government at all levels.

Jefferson also sought to physically expand the United States as part of his vision of an America populated by farmers from sea to sea. The problem was that all of the land west of the Mississippi River was claimed by the British, French, or Spanish as well as numerous American Indian tribes.

Since Jefferson and the Democratic–Republicans favored France, even when it was ruled by Napoleon, Jefferson sent James Monroe and Robert Livingston to France in 1803 to negotiate for control of New Orleans.

They came back to America with 828,000 more square miles in what is known as the Louisiana Purchase. The purchase of what would become most of the Great Plains states, parts of the upper Midwest states, and parts of the Rocky Mountain states, came at a whopping price of $15 million, which in today's prices would be a little more than $1 trillion!

Needless to say, the fiscally conservative Federalists weren't happy with the price tag and opposed the purchase. However, by that time, their influence was greatly diminished and the treaty granting the land to the United States was ratified by both houses of Congress.

As discussed earlier in this book, the Lewis and Clark expedition quickly followed the Louisiana Purchase, bringing a wave of American settlement to the west. It was all made possible through Jefferson's vision.

A CONTINUING LEGACY

Like many of the heroes profiled in this book, Thomas Jefferson was a complex person full of many apparent contradictions. He was a slave owner who theoretically opposed slavery and signed a law that made the international slave trade illegal.

He had a deep respect for many Native American tribes, yet he thought that they were standing in the way of his vision for America. He theoretically opposed the expansion of the central government, yet had no problem using it to expand the size of the United States.

With all of that said, there is no denying that Thomas Jefferson is a true American hero.

Jefferson risked his freedom and liberty by supporting the American Revolution and ensuring that future generations would have the freedom and liberty to question the government.

He eloquently articulated in writing why people are born free and that, although there may be limits on what the government should do, there are very few limits on what free people can do. Thomas Jefferson also increased the number of people involved in government, opening the door for true democracy in the United States.

There is no doubt that Thomas Jefferson had a profound influence on the United States that continues today in many ways.

DID YOU KNOW?

- Thomas Jefferson was a bibliophile, building three separate personal libraries during his lifetime. His third library was the largest, with over 20,000 volumes.

- Like Benjamin Franklin, Thomas Jefferson was also an inventor. Among the more useful and interesting of his inventions was a polygraph, which was a device that could instantly make copies of a document as you wrote it.

- He married his wife Martha in 1772 and, although they were only married for ten years before she died, they had six children.

- Jefferson was also an accomplished architect, favoring the neo-classical style. He designed the mansion at his primary Virginia home, which he named Monticello.

- Jefferson could speak and write the modern languages of French, Italian, Greek, and German as well as the ancient languages of classical Greek, Latin, and Anglo-Saxon. He later learned some American Indian languages in his dealings with American Indian leaders.

CHARLES LINDBERGH
HERO OF AMERICAN AVIATION

The Wright Brothers were first in flight, but it was Charles Lindbergh who demonstrated to the world the practicality of the new mode of transportation. Risking his life, Lindbergh was one of the nation's first air-mail carriers and, most famously, became the first person to fly solo across the Atlantic Ocean.

Lindbergh's success in the skies showed the world what was possible and, in doing so, he captured the imagination and hearts of millions of Americans.

The tall, handsome, and blond Lucky Lindy—as he was known when he became a media sensation in the 1920s and '30s—was one of America's first victims of the paparazzi.

Although the son of a wealthy and connected U.S. Congressman, life was not always easy for Lindbergh. He was a man who pushed the limits, which almost cost him his life on more than one occasion. He also lost one of his children to a bizarre kidnapping plot turned murder.

The murder of his child made him into a bit of a recluse for a while, but he returned to public life in the late 1930s.

Lindbergh wore many hats throughout his life: political

activist, inventor, and environmentalist. However, it was his work in aviation that made him a true American hero. Lindbergh showed that long-distance flight was not only possible but was something that could be possible for other people, too.

After Lindbergh made his famed trans-Atlantic flight in 1927, it opened the skies for regular air travel within 20 years.

LUCKY LINDY

Charles Augustus Lindbergh was born in Detroit, Michigan in 1902 to Charles and Evangeline Lindbergh. Although the senior Lindbergh would be quite successful in life, serving five terms as a U.S. Congressman from Minnesota, he was the product of an illicit affair in Sweden. After Charles Senior was born, his parents essentially fled to Minnesota for a new start.

So, although Charles was born into a good position, there was a lingering mark on the Lindbergh family that occasionally reared its head. For the most part, though, young Charles had a fairly good early life. He was primarily raised in Minnesota, but as a congressman's son, he spent quite a bit of time in Washington and was enrolled in numerous boarding schools.

Largely because he was constantly on the move, young Charles never had many childhood friends and was often on guard with people throughout his life. This led Charles to focus more on his inherent intellectual talents, of which he had many.

Charles had an early interest in science and mechanics and worked on his family's car and his own motorbike as a teenager. Between his father's influence and his good grades in school, Charles had many colleges to choose from, but he chose to stay close to home and attend the University of Wisconsin–Madison.

He initially entered the mechanical engineering program at Wisconsin–Madison with great enthusiasm, but quickly found the course work stifling and too easy. Charles wanted to experience life, in particular flying, and he wasn't going to be able to do that in a classroom.

Even if he graduated early, he would still have to spend about three years studying, which was just too much for Lindbergh. To the surprise and consternation of his parents, Lindbergh dropped out of college after one semester to attend a flight school in Lincoln, Nebraska in 1922.

You probably noticed that Lindbergh followed a similar pattern to the other scientific heroes in our book. Most of America's scientific heroes had little formal education, but thanks to a combination of natural intelligence and intellectual freedom, they were able to thrive and become the heroes we know them as today.

Charles Lindbergh was given the freedom to explore and create and he certainly had the intelligence to be a success.

After earning his pilot license, Lindbergh traveled through the South and Midwest on several barnstorming tours. During these, he and other pilots would wow local crowds by performing death-defying stunts, such as walking on the wings of their planes or flying them through empty barns.

It was certainly dangerous work, but since he was an aviation pioneer, it raised Lindbergh's public profile and brought him to the attention of the United States Army. He joined the

Army's flying corps when there were few capable instructors; in fact, Lindbergh was probably a better pilot than most of his Army instructors!

It was while he was training in the Army in 1925 that he first earned the moniker Lucky Lindy. He was involved in a mid-air collision that forced him to parachute to safety. Despite the collision, Lindbergh graduated at the top of his class.

There were still many adventures in store for Lucky Lindy.

THE SPIRIT OF ST. LOUIS

Not long after he graduated from the Army pilot training, Lindbergh made another big step in his life when he joined the United States Postal Service as one of the first air-mail postmen. This would turn out to be a major move forward in this country as well.

His job was to fly an irregularly scheduled route from St. Louis to Chicago and back. Since aviation was still a new technology, the job came with quite a few hazards, which Lindbergh faced twice in 1926.

Lindbergh's first close call came on a rainy night in September, outside of Chicago. He flew into a thunderstorm as he approached Chicago. After flying blind for some time, he was forced to parachute to safety.

Then, about six weeks later, Lindbergh ran into bad weather again in central Illinois and had to bail from his plane. On both occasions, Lindbergh was more concerned about the condition of his planes and locating the lost mail than he was with his safety.

Perhaps at that point he believed that he was Lucky Lindy and that he couldn't be hurt. More than likely, he was focused on attaining his dream of flying across the Atlantic Ocean.

Lindbergh planned to enter the competition for the Orteig Prize in 1927, but he had several barriers in his way. The Orteig Prize was a $25,000 prize that was to be awarded by tycoon Raymond Orteig to the first person who could fly solo from New York to Paris or Paris to New York.

Although two Brits—John Alcock and Arthur Whitten Brown—successfully flew from Newfoundland to Ireland in 1919 in a World War I plane, the Orteig Prize was for a much longer flight and had to be done solo. Several pilots crashed and burned and two were lost over the Atlantic attempting to achieve the feat.

Fear wasn't something Lindbergh considered, so finance was the main barrier.

Lucky Lindy had the technical ability to design a plane himself, but he needed money to do so. Lindbergh used some of his Midwestern charms to wrangle some money from a couple of St. Louis businessmen.

Along with some money he had saved, this was enough to build the legendary plane known as the *Spirit of St. Louis*. He began building the plane in early 1927 in California and by May it was ready to go.

The single-seat plane was designed like nothing before it—or since, for that matter. It had to be big enough to carry more than 400 gallons of fuel and a 5,000-pound engine. The navigational devices were minimal and there was no radio equipment on board, so Lindbergh primarily used dead reckoning. There was also no window in the front of the plane.

It can't be stressed enough just how dangerous Lindbergh's trip was. If he went down in the ocean, there would've been no rescue effort. He may as well have been flying into outer space because he had no safety net. It was just him, his plane, and the ocean.

Lucky Lindy left New York on May 20, 1927 and just over 33 hours later he arrived in Paris to a jubilant crowd of more than 150,000 people. The trip was harrowing, with weather almost putting him in the ocean on multiple occasions, but Lindbergh once more lived up to his nickname.

Charles Lindbergh proved what man was capable of and it made every American proud that he was one of their own.

A NATIONAL HERO

Charles Lindbergh was never a guy who desired celebrity, and with his fame came plenty of tragedy and controversy. He toured the world, speaking about his monumental flight, and became as wealthy as he was famous. Lindbergh's fame and wealth played a role in the kidnapping and murder of his 20-month-old son, Charles Junior, in 1932 in New Jersey. Devasted by the murder, Lindbergh moved his family to Europe for several years.

Lindbergh did not retire from working; in fact, he expanded his activities into other fields.

During the 1930s, he invented an artificial heart pump that—although primitive by later standards—allowed for open-heart surgeries to become a reality.

Among the more controversial aspects of Lindbergh's life was his stance on politics. With the prospect of another world war looking more and more like a reality by the mid-1930s, Lindbergh did what he could to keep the United States out of the war.

Driven partly by anti-communist ideology, partly by respect for Germany, and partly by American isolationism, Lindbergh became one of the more recognized figures in the America First Committee, which was a private organization dedicated to keeping the United States out of World War II.

Lindbergh's political activism put him at odds with President Roosevelt, who referred to the aviation hero as an *"appeaser."*

Once the United States entered the war, though, Lindbergh ended his activism and applied his aviation skills to the war in the Pacific Theater. Lindbergh worked with the Navy and the Marines as a civilian consultant but ended up flying several combat missions, plus helped increase the fuel efficiency of American planes.

AN IMPACTFUL LIFE

Perhaps knowing that many people would view him as a bit of a relic or a dinosaur from a different era, Lindbergh all but retired from the public eye once more after the war. He was a dedicated conservationist, but he shied away from controversial ideas, or anything political, for that matter.

By the time Lindbergh died in 1974 in Hawaii, America had changed dramatically from when he made his famous 1927 flight.

Lindbergh played a major role in many of those technological changes during those 50 years. When Lindbergh flew the

Spirit of St. Louis across the Atlantic, he showed the world not only what was possible, but how it could be done.

He blazed a brave new trail in the world, opening the way for regular air travel, which ultimately led to several other scientific discoveries and inventions.

Lindbergh may have been lucky, but he was also quite skilled and daring. Because of those traits, he is one of America's greatest heroes of the 20th century.

DID YOU KNOW?

- Lindbergh married his wife Anne in 1929 and the couple had six children. In recent years, historians revealed that Lindbergh carried on lengthy affairs with three German women after World War II, fathering a further seven children between the women.

- A total of six men died trying to win the Orteig Prize.

- The *Spirit of St. Louis* was modeled after a Ryan M-2 airplane. The plane was assembled at the Ryan Aircraft hangar in San Diego, California.

- When Charles Junior was kidnapped, the Lindbergh family paid a ransom, but he was murdered anyway. The kidnapper, Richard Hauptmann, was captured, convicted, and executed for what became known as the *"crime of the century."*

- Lindbergh wrote seven books on topics ranging from his life experiences to engineering and aviation.

JACKIE ROBINSON
BARRIER-BREAKING HERO

We've seen how a couple of athletes became American heroes by defining their sports. Babe Ruth and Jim Thorpe certainly changed the way baseball and football were played, respectively, and accomplished success in the face of great adversity. Jackie Robinson was also an American professional athlete who defined a sport—but also an era—by breaking the color barrier to become the first African American to play in Major League Baseball.

Jackie Robinson accomplished that feat when segregation was still legal and the law of the land in many states. Racial discrimination was common in the states where legal segregation wasn't practiced.

Robinson was successful not because he was some type of social experiment or political pawn, but because he was a legitimately excellent player. Lost beneath the long-term social and political ramifications of Robinson integrating Major League Baseball is the fact that he was one of the best players of his era.

Robinson was the National League rookie of the year in 1947, a six-time Major League All-Star, the 1949 National League

MVP, and was inducted into the Baseball Hall of Fame on the first ballot in 1962.

Of course, the fact that Robinson had to deal with so much adversity off the field made his on the field accomplishments that much more impressive. Yet, it was on the field where he made the most difference.

To say that there was resistance to Robinson playing in the Majors would be an understatement. When it was announced that Robinson was moving from the Negro Leagues to the Majors, many White Americans were upset by what it could signal.

Meanwhile, many Black Americans looked to him as a symbol of their hopes. After Robinson arrived to play for the Brooklyn Dodgers, he faced resistance from some of his teammates and many of the tough New York fans.

But it didn't take long for Jackie Robinson to win over New York and the rest of America. By the end of his rookie season, Jackie had become a legitimate hero for Black *and* White Americans. He was the true American success story — a living example of how hard work and talent can raise a person above adversity. Perhaps most importantly, Jackie Robinson accomplished everything with dignity and a great attitude.

For all of those reasons, Robinson is the only major league player who has had his number — 42 — retired by every team in the Majors.

A NATURAL ATHLETE

Jackie Robinson was born in 1919 in racially segregated Georgia and grew up primarily in southern California, which was also quite segregated. Fortunately for young Jackie, he had a solid family foundation to support him and some good genes. Athletic ability ran in the Robinson family, as Jackie's older brother Mack won a silver medal in the 200-meter race at the 1936 Summer Olympics. Mack not only provided Jackie with an example of athletic excellence, he also encouraged his younger brother's sports activities and kept him out of trouble.

Jackie was a high school sports star, starting for his school's football, basketball, baseball, and track teams. Although baseball would be the sport for which he became famous, Robinson was known more for being a track star in college.

While he was at UCLA in the early 1940s, Jackie began his legacy of breaking barriers by being one of only four Black players on the football team and winning the long jump in track and field.

Robinson left school before graduating. Just as he was considering returning to earn his diploma, the Japanese bombed Pearl Harbor. The attack led the United States into World War II and most of the nation's young, healthy men were drafted into service, including Robinson.

It was in the military where Robinson came face-to-face with some of the cold realities of racial segregation.

The segregation Jackie faced in southern California was a lot less apparent and assertive than what he experienced in the military. Sure, there were neighborhoods in and around Los

Angeles where he could get into trouble with the locals, or the police, for entering, but those places were fairly easy to avoid. In the Army, though, it was marked where he could and couldn't go. Blacks served in all Black units, but most of their officers were White.

Jackie met boxing superstar Joe Louis in the Army and, together, the two men petitioned for more Black officers. Robinson eventually made lieutenant, but he was nearly drummed out when he refused to move to the back of an Army commuter bus. An all-White jury found him not guilty of insubordination, but Robinson knew that the Army was no place for him.

As much as Jackie Robinson may have wanted to change the way things were at that point in his life, he was newly engaged and was thinking about his future family first. He never thought of himself as an activist, but he knew he was an athlete.

So, Robinson did as any athlete in his position would do: he played sports!

FROM THE NEGRO LEAGUES TO THE MAJORS

Most professional sports doors were closed to Jackie Robinson in 1945. He coached for a short time before landing a contract with the Kansas City Monarch of the Negro American League. At that time, the Negro Leagues were the only possibility for most players of color.

Some Hispanics played in the Major leagues, but there were no African Americans in either the American or National leagues. So, of course, the Negro Leagues had some pretty good players.

Still, for Jackie, it just wasn't the same. The pay wasn't as good and there was less prestige. Almost immediately, he began actively looking for a spot on a Major League team.

It wasn't that there was a law against Blacks playing on Major League teams, or even that there was a rule in the Majors prohibiting Black players. The owners tended to follow the norms of society at the time, which dictated a clear racial barrier in many things, baseball being one of them. Jackie trained hard for his big shot, but no matter how hard he trained, a team needed to take a chance on him.

Branch Rickey was the general manager of the Brooklyn Dodgers (yes, they were in New York for quite a while before moving to Los Angeles in 1958). He was seen as a brilliant guy when it came to baseball management and business.

He had a natural gift for locating talent and, in 1945, that included recruiting the best from the Negro Leagues. After seeing Jackie play and try out for the Dodgers, Rickey was impressed, but he was even more impressed after talking to him.

The Dodgers signed Robinson to a lucrative $600 a month contract, which was immediately followed by pushback. Resistance was certainly expected, but Robinson was a little surprised that the first wave of opposition came from other Negro League players.

Some other Negro League players argued that Robinson wasn't even the best Negro League player and that others deserved a shot before him. The reality is that Robinson was just one of several Negro League players who was signed to a contract. He just happened to be the first to get called up from the minor leagues.

Jackie played one season for the Dodgers' minor league team, the Montreal Royals. It was with the Royals in spring training that Jackie got a taste of the segregation that was still quite common throughout the South.

He was often forced to stay in and sometimes even train in different facilities than his team. Still, despite the obvious distractions, he made it through the season and was called up for the Dodgers for the 1947 season.

Robinson's first year in the Majors would be a true test of his mental toughness.

Although there was some initial tension in the Dodger's clubhouse when Jackie joined the team, his teammates quickly accepted him. They soon had his back in on the field conflicts with other players.

And there were certainly a few conflicts over Robinson's breaking of the color line.

The Dodgers players and fans quickly accepted Robinson, even if some did so begrudgingly. It was the fans and players from the Dodgers' rival teams — such as St. Louis, Boston, and Philadelphia — who had the most to say. Rival fans shouted racial slurs at Jackie from the stands, as did more than a few players on the field, as well as sliding in hard with their cleats up against the infielder.

But Jackie persisted and never let the abuse get to him. Or, at least, he never let it show, which is more than most people would've been capable of. Not only that, but Robinson also recorded such good numbers that he won the National League rookie of the year honors.

A LIFE THAT TRANSCENDED BASEBALL

Jackie Robinson would go on to live a fulfilling life after he retired from baseball in 1956. He became politically active in the civil rights movement and supported candidates from both major political parties. Robinson also became the first Black person to analyze Major League baseball games on television in 1965.

But there is little doubt that Jackie Robinson will also be remembered for being a sports hero, particularly as the man who broke the color barrier in Major League baseball. Someone had to be the first, so Jackie Robinson stepped up to the plate to take the abuse that allowed him and other Black players to have a chance in the Majors.

Jackie Robinson may have been a great athlete, but what he did on and off the diamond truly transcended sports and is what made him a true American hero.

DID YOU KNOW?

- Despite being a professional athlete and in good shape for most of his life, Jackie died in 1972, at the age of 53, of a heart attack. He had suffered from diabetes for several years.

- Jackie married his wife Rachel in 1946. The couple had two sons and one daughter. The couple's oldest son, Jackie Junior, died in a car accident a few months before Jackie died.

- Robinson's middle name was Roosevelt. Jackie's father left the family not long after he was born, so his mother was forced to raise him and his four siblings on her own.

- Jackie stood at 5'11", which was a good size for the era, especially for an infielder. He had a .311 lifetime batting average and, although not much of a power hitter, led the National League twice in stolen bases.

- In 1949, Robinson testified at the House Un-American Activities Committee in Washington about his relationship with fellow Black athlete Paul Robeson. Although Robinson was never under suspicion, Robeson was later blacklisted for having communist sympathies.

JOHN WAYNE
HERO OF THE AMERICAN SILVER SCREEN

Our book so far has covered a wide swath of heroes from American history, including sports, political, and scientific heroes. We've also looked at a few anti-heroes. So, now let's take a look at America's greatest *"pretend"* hero — John Wayne.

Although John Wayne died in 1979, there are few adults alive today who haven't heard his name. You may not be able to name one of his movies off-hand, but when you hear the name, the image of the Duke dressed as a cowboy probably comes to mind. That endurance is a testament to John Wayne's influence on American culture and part of what makes him an American hero.

John Wayne rose to Hollywood fame long before the public was bombarded by social media posts of self-important actors who are here today and gone tomorrow. It was a time when actors had to present an image off-screen that coincided with their on-screen personalities, even if it was a sham.

For John Wayne, his on-screen persona as a rough and tough true-blue American male was, for the most part, true to his personal life. He was symbolic of a different time in America, which became especially true during the 1960s.

Because John Wayne represented stability and traditional American values, he became the most popular American film actor from the 1940s through to the 1960s. John Wayne was also a true ironman of the cinema, appearing in more than 170 films throughout his long career.

Although today many see John Wayne's films and acting as corny, there is no denying that he greatly influenced American film and continues to do so, as his movies are still shown regularly on television and are available on all streaming services.

MARION ROBERT MORRISON

As much as John Wayne was, and is still, associated with American masculinity, his life began with a decidedly non-traditionally masculine sounding name—Marion Morrison.

Morrison was born to a middle-class family in 1907 in Iowa and raised in southern California during the period of its initial boom. Hollywood was burgeoning into a major institution with the emergence of silent films. People were moving there from all over the country to make it big.

Marion didn't have any dreams of film stardom as he grew up, although he did show promise in several fields. The extremely gregarious Morrison made friends easily, and due to his charisma became the president of many school clubs. He was an excellent student and a natural-born athlete, which earned him a football scholarship to the University of Southern California in the late 1920s.

Everything seemed to be going well for the future film star. After all, it was the 1920s, the economy was doing well, and it was a period of peace between the world wars. People had time to enjoy themselves, which the young Morrison did by going to parties, dating, and even surfing.

The athletic Morrison tried just about any sport, but his flirtation with surfing nearly cost him his future when he was injured. The injury forced him off the USC football team and out of school, but fate stepped in to push the young man in a different direction.

Howard Jones, USC's football coach at the time, thought he'd do Morrison a favor by introducing him to some Hollywood people.

He thought maybe they could get him a job working on sets. Marion was hired for behind-the-scenes work, but the young man's 6'4" frame and rugged good looks impressed directors so much that he quickly became an extra. He then landed several small film roles in the early 1930s.

Morrison had the looks, a commanding stage presence, and had no problem remembering his lines; there was just one problem, though—his name!

BECOMING THE DUKE

Hollywood has been a superficial, shallow place, where one's success is often based on looks or voice. Marion Morrison developed his signature gravelly voice pretty early from hanging around legendary lawman Wyatt Earp. His name, though, just wasn't going to cut it when the credits rolled.

For Marion, his birth name wasn't a problem. In fact, despite being known globally as John Wayne, and although his children took that name, he never legally changed his name.

But Hollywood is a superficial place, so if some directors decided that Marion Morrison wasn't going to cut it, then it had to be changed.

Morrison had gone by the nickname Duke since he was a child. Duke was the name of his childhood dog; as he and the dog were inseparable, people in his neighborhood began calling him Duke.

Well, Duke sounded pretty masculine and cool, but *"Duke Morrison"* still wasn't working so, after some deliberation, the directors eventually gave him the name John Wayne. It was simple, tough-sounding, and very American. It would be perfect for a future superstar.

John Wayne earned several minor and supporting film roles throughout the 1930s, but it was the 1939 film *Stagecoach* that set him on the road to stardom.

Stagecoach was a Western directed by the famous John Ford. It was a formulaic Western, complete with bad guys versus good guys, but it helped establish the genre in American cinema and John Wayne as an A-list actor.

Although best known for the countless Westerns he starred in, Wayne also got top billing in plenty of war movies, including *Sands of Iwo Jima* (1949), *The Longest Day* (1962), and *The Green Berets* (1968). He also starred in some dramas, made cameos in movies, and appeared on countless celebrity roasts and talk shows.

During the height of his acting career in the 1950s, Wayne stepped behind the cameras to produce many movies, finding success in that aspect of the film industry, most notably with *The Alamo* (1960).

Wayne won the Academy Award for best actor in 1970 for his role in the film *True Grit* and received numerous other awards throughout his career.

Wayne was diagnosed with lung cancer in 1964. After successfully beating the disease, he went against the advice of his agent and Hollywood industry insiders by going public with his disease and urging people to get tested.

A TRUE AMERICAN ICON

By the time John Wayne died of cancer in 1979, he was a fixed part of the American cultural landscape. His movies were known throughout the world; even in the otherwise closed Soviet Union, John Wayne films were popular.

He represented a pioneer American spirit that was — for the most part — already gone by the time he became a film star. Yet, still enough of it was left lingering for his films to resonate with Americans.

John Wayne became a hero for Americans from coast to coast because he represented the man who most men wanted to be, and most women wanted to be with.

He may have been a product or a reflection of the United States in the mid-20th century, but at the same time, there is no denying that he influenced American culture.

As corny as John Wayne's movies and acting style may seem to many people today, his films are still regularly shown and will likely continue to be for future generations, ensuring that he is America's greatest hero of the silver screen.

DID YOU KNOW?

- John Wayne was married three times and had seven children. All three of his wives were of Hispanic heritage.

- Wayne was an open and vocal conservative, which earned him a few enemies in generally liberal Hollywood. This is a reason some people point to for reassessing his hero status. Some of his racial views, in particular, are considered very outdated today.

- During the 1950s and '60s, John Wayne was in such high demand that he turned down many big roles. One role that he didn't turn down, though, was as Marshal Matt Dillon in the long-running television series *Gunsmoke*. The urban legend originated because Wayne recommended James Arness for the role. Wayne also introduced the pilot episode of the series, but he was making too much money as an A-lister to have done television at that point in his career.

- Wayne was a heavy smoker and drinker throughout his life. The smoking probably contributed to his cancer and the drinking made him difficult to work with at times. Directors tried to shoot his scenes before noon because after that point he was said to turn into a mean drunk.

- Wayne starred as the Mongol conqueror Genghis Khan in the forgettable 1956 *The Conqueror*. Although the film was a flop, it became widely known because 91 of the cast and crew of 220 got cancer, with 46, including Wayne, dying from some form of the disease. The film was shot in rural Utah, downwind from a nuclear weapon test site in Nevada.

AMELIA EARHART
FLYING THROUGH THE GLASS CEILING

We've examined the lives of some pretty amazing women in this book who can be considered true American heroines by any account. They blazed trails and contributed in many different ways to the country that we have today.

Susan B. Anthony is notable for actively pursuing the cause of women's suffrage and feminism in general, but if there was one woman in American who truly lived the life that Anthony spoke about, it was Amelia Earhart.

You probably know a little about Amelia Earhart's tragic 1937 flight around the world, where she and her navigator disappeared when they were nearing the end of their more than 27,000-mile flight. It wouldn't have been the first flight around the world, but it would've been the longest, as it followed an equatorial route.

Earhart and her navigator Fred Noonan were lost somewhere in the South Pacific with no trace, leaving behind one of the modern world's greatest mysteries and making Earhart an enduring legend in the process.

But Amelia Earhart was so much more than that tragic flight.

Amelia had been living a life of independence for decades

before her voyage around the world, shattering numerous glass ceilings and blazing many trails in the process.

She became the first woman to fly solo across the Atlantic Ocean, was the first person to fly solo from Honolulu to Oakland, raced planes competitively, was a published author, and taught aeronautics at the university level when no other women were doing so.

The fact that Earhart was able to do so much in her 39 years makes her death that much more tragic because she was truly an incredible woman who deeply impacted American history.

A TOMBOY FULL OF LIFE

When Amelia Earhart was a girl in the early 1900s, the word *"tomboy"* was a standard way to describe girls who had interests in traditionally masculine things. Born in 1897 in Kansas, Amelia's family moved around the Midwest quite a bit for her father's work with the railroads, so she and her younger sister Grace became quite close.

The two girls enjoyed what were traditionally considered boy pursuits, such as hiking, fishing, and shooting. And perhaps even a little more risqué for the time, the girls preferred to wear bloomers instead of dresses.

When Amelia wasn't doing these activities with her sister, she was constantly reading whatever books she could find in the family home or the local library. Perhaps because she had a difficult time fitting in with other kids, Amelia also spent a lot of her time daydreaming about a career other than as a housewife. She knew that the world was a big place and she wanted to see and experience as much of it as possible.

After graduating from high school, the restless Earhart traveled around North America for several years. She worked as a nurse in Toronto, Ontario for a few months, where she saw first-hand the ravages of war with the soldiers returning from World War I.

She also briefly enrolled in college with the intent of studying medicine but quit—not because the curriculum was too difficult—but because the idea of being stuck in a classroom was too stifling for the free-spirited young woman.

After moving to California to live with her parents in 1920, Amelia was introduced to aviation and never looked back.

EARNING HER WINGS

Earhart began taking flying lessons in 1921 and earned her pilot's license in 1923, becoming one of only 16 women at the time to have done so. Things certainly seemed to be looking up for Amelia in the 1920s, but then a series of unfortunate events nearly ended her flying career.

Financial problems led Amelia to sell the plane she had bought with inheritance money, and sinus problems she incurred also threatened to ground her aviation plans.

But Earhart persevered and continued to nurture her love of flying, while living in the Boston area. After having an operation for her sinus problems, the mild ocean breezes of Boston seemed to do wonders for her health and spirits. Plus, the people of the area were more than receptive to a female aviator.

In 1928, she flew with a copilot from Newfoundland, Canada to Wales, becoming the first woman to make the transatlantic flight. Although it certainly was an admirable feat, Earhart knew there was so much more she could do, so she began preparing for a solo flight across the Atlantic.

On May 20, 1932, Earhart made the nearly 15-hour flight from Newfoundland to Northern Ireland, becoming the first woman to fly solo across the Atlantic Ocean. The already fairly well-known Earhart became a major celebrity in the United States, bringing her fame and wealth.

She was offered endorsements and book deals and was invited to lecture at a variety of different organizations. Most importantly, she was taken seriously by her peers, male and female, in the aviation world.

Many people made comparisons between Earhart and Charles Lindbergh. After all, they were both important American aviators, and Earhart's tall, lean, Nordic appearance could have made her Lindbergh's sister.

Earhart was flattered by the comparison, but at the same time, she wanted to be known for her accomplishments — and obviously, there were plenty. So, in 1936, she began planning her fateful expedition around the world.

Just as Lindbergh did for his monumental voyage, Earhart had a plane built to her specifications in California. As an example of how quickly technology had progressed since Lindbergh built the *Spirit of St. Louis*, Lockheed constructed Earhart's modified Model 10 Electra twin-engine plane in just one month.

After an aborted attempt to do the journey beginning by crossing the Pacific Ocean, Earhart and Noonan left Miami, Florida on June 1, 1937, and then weaved their way in a southeasterly direction through South America, Africa and, finally, into New Guinea.

The trip had already been a month-long at that point, but they were coming to the last and most dangerous leg. After they left New Guinea on July 2, they were to go in a northeasterly direction, eventually reaching Hawaii and then turning east for the continental United States.

Their next stop was supposed to be the lonely Howland Island in the middle of the South Pacific, but they never made it.

The United States Navy sent out search and rescue crews for Earhart and Noonan, but no trace of them or the airplane was ever found.

A HEROINE WHEN THE COUNTRY NEEDED IT

Amelia Earhart's disappearance and presumed death in the South Pacific came as a blow to millions of Americans who were following her journey. People had come to love the trailblazing female pilot because she gave everyone something to believe in and rally around during the tough years of the Great Depression.

Earhart showed millions of American girls and women that they, too, could push the limits if they set their minds and hearts to it. In the decades after her disappearance and presumed death, women fighting for equal rights in the workplace often used Amelia Earhart as an example of true equality and the independent spirit of the American woman.

Amelia Earhart continues to inspire people today to follow

their dreams, no matter how lofty they may seem. For that reason, she is a true American heroine.

DID YOU KNOW?

- The most credible theory regarding Earhart's disappearance is that she ran out of fuel and had to ditch the plane. She and Noonan then drifted in the ocean for a while before drowning. Another theory holds that the pair made it to an uninhabited island before dying. A more outlandish theory is that Earhart was somehow captured and later killed by Japanese soldiers on one of the Japanese held islands, such as Saipan.

- Earhart married American book publisher George Putnam in 1931. They remained married until Earhart's disappearance and presumed death.

- Earhart was an outspoken feminist and early supporter of the Equal Rights Amendment, although she dedicated most of her feminist energies toward helping women aviators instead of lobbying legislators.

- Amelia joined the Ninety-Nines, a female pilot organization before she made her solo flight across the Atlantic.

- Earhart competed in several long-distance air races in the 1930s, but the planes she flew never did too well against the specially built racers.

SEQUOYAH
BRINGING LITERACY TO HIS PEOPLE

Earlier in this book, we explored the incredible life of American Indian leader Sitting Bull. He was a hero to his people for fighting the American government, but also later became a hero to White Americans because of his bravery and stoic acceptance of the situation.

When most people think of great American Indian heroes, if Sitting Bull isn't the first one to come to mind, it is usually another warrior chieftain.

But there was so much more to Native American culture than warfare. There were several peaceful heroes to emerge from the numerous tribes, the most important of whom was the Cherokee leader and scholar Sequoyah.

Sequoyah created a syllabic alphabet for the Cherokee language, which was a monumental task when one considers history and what it takes to accomplish such a feat.

Most forms of writing evolve over time and are only gradually linked to a spoken language. For instance, the alphabet used in the written English language — and nearly all Western European languages — is the Latin alphabet.

The Latin alphabet was developed by the Romans who got the

idea of writing from the Greeks. The Greeks developed their alphabet based on Phoenician writing, which came directly from the ancient Canaanites. The Canaanites developed their form of writing independently, although there were probably influences from Egypt and Mesopotamia.

So, you see, a writing form/alphabet can take hundreds or even thousands of years to fully develop, but Sequoyah developed the Cherokee syllabary in about a year.

Thanks in large part to Sequoyah's efforts, the Cherokee have historically been one of the most successful American Indian tribes. Despite being physically moved from their homeland in the southeastern United States and placed in Oklahoma, the Cherokee built schools and businesses on their way to becoming politically important in the state of Oklahoma.

Since Sequoyah introduced the Cherokee syllabary to his people, Cherokee literacy rates have been on similar levels to that of their White neighbors. Cherokee levels of crime, unemployment, and alcoholism have been much lower than that of other American Indian tribes.

Of course, several factors have played a role in the Cherokee's success, but at the center of it all is Sequoyah and his efforts to bring literacy to his people.

GEORGE GIST

Sequoyah was born just before the American Revolution (around 1770) in the Cherokee village near what is today Knoxville, Tennessee. His mother was Cherokee, and his father was probably White, which allowed him to travel a bit in both worlds, although he was seen and identified as Cherokee.

He was given the English name George Gist, but he became best known for his Cherokee name, Sequoyah.

The Cherokee were generally considered a friendly tribe by the British, after their arrival in North America. When the American Revolution broke out, most Cherokees joined the American side.

Unfortunately, due to a lack of proper records, there are few details about Sequoyah's early life. It is known that as an adult he had a limp, but when and how that happened has been a source of debate. One story is that he received a wound in the War of 1812 fighting against Britain's Indian allies, while other sources suggest that he was injured as a child.

Sequoyah received no formal schooling, but he always displayed an inquisitiveness and mechanical aptitude. He made a living as a farmer and a silversmith and, on the side, he repaired and made tools for his neighbors.

Since his people usually had friendly relations with Whites, he was introduced to modern European technology at an early age. Sequoyah used many of those tools in his silversmith and merchant businesses, but the one technology that amazed him the most was writing.

In the early 1800s, as the Cherokee were being quickly enveloped by White settlement in the southeast, Sequoyah knew that the only way his people would survive in the long-term was by learning the *"talking leaves,"* as he called writing. Sequoyah was an intelligent, forward-looking man: he knew that education, not warfare, would be the key to survival. So, in 1809, he set out to devise a written alphabet for the Cherokee language.

BUILDING THE CHEROKEE NATION

What makes Sequoyah's invention of the Cherokee alphabet so phenomenal is that he knew little English and had only a cursory knowledge of writing. Because Sequoyah had no background in philology, he struggled at first to create a Cherokee alphabet and system of writing.

He at first envisioned an idiomatic system, where there would be a symbol for each word in the Cherokee language, but when that proved too unwieldy, he attempted to create a symbol for every idea. Of course, that idea also proved to be too burdensome.

After doing some research on modern European languages, Sequoyah learned that modern alphabets are syllabic/phonetic, with each letter representing a distinct sound. He knew that such an alphabet could also be devised for Cherokee after a finite number of sounds were determined.

Sequoyah found that the Cherokee language had about 100 sounds that could be put into writing with 86 characters, so the next step in his project was determining those characters/ letters.

Since English was the written language that Sequoyah saw the most, the Latin alphabet was the inspiration for most of the Cherokee writing system, although Greek, Cyrillic, and entirely new letters were also used.

One of the most interesting aspects of the Cherokee syllabary is that, since Sequoyah didn't know how to read English, most letters in Cherokee don't correspond to a similar sound in the Latin alphabet.

Sequoyah immediately presented his new script to Cherokee leaders, who readily accepted the system. A Cherokee language newspaper soon followed and official documents were written in Cherokee in the southeastern Cherokee lands as well as in Indian Territory (roughly equivalent to modern-day Oklahoma).

Cherokee leaders pointed to the Cherokee syllabary as an example of their civilized status to stop their removal from the southeast to Indian Territory. Despite this, the removals began in earnest in 1830.

As traumatizing and tragic as the period of American Indian removal was for the Cherokee in the southeast, thanks to Sequoyah and his writing system, there was a semblance of order when they arrived in Indian Territory.

THE POWER OF LITERACY

Because the modern world is literate, the power of literacy is often taken for granted. Most of us learn how to read even before we begin school, which is followed shortly after by writing. If you think about it, it would be nearly impossible to have a modern, civilized society without writing.

Written records are required for record-keeping and writing is how most societies pass down their religion, history, and culture from one generation to another. Writing is also how some of history's most creative minds have expressed themselves.

When Europeans first began to clash with the indigenous tribes of North America, the Europeans had many clear technological advantages. Many think that the guns and cannons of the

Europeans were the prime advantage but writing played an equal role in their eventual dominance over the continent.

Cherokee leader Sequoyah knew that writing and literacy was the only way his people would survive the onslaught of manifest destiny.

Sequoyah knew that the Cherokee couldn't hope to defeat the Americans on the battlefield, but if they learned the knowledge of writing, then they had more than a fighting chance at survival. And, for the most part, history has proven Sequoyah correct.

Despite all of the obstacles and tribulations the Cherokee faced, they developed into the model upon which all other American Indian tribes aspire. It is mostly due to Sequoyah that they were the first tribe to become widely literate.

DID YOU KNOW?

- Sequoyah was married twice and had seven children.

- Like many other American Indians, Sequoyah struggled with alcoholism early in his adulthood. He eventually beat alcoholism, though, by dedicating most of his time to his business and other interests, such as the Cherokee syllabary.

- The Cherokee syllabary was not a simple system. Many of the letters represented consonant-vowel combinations. The first Cherokee language document Sequoyah wrote dealt with the boundaries of the Cherokee Nation in the southeast.

- Sequoyah was living in what is now northern Alabama when he developed the Cherokee syllabary. He was one of the first Cherokee to move to Indian Territory in 1825.

- Like Amelia Earhart, Sequoyah disappeared and was eventually presumed dead. He left Indian Territory in 1842 to find lost bands of Cherokee who fled to Mexico during the period of American Indian removal. Most people believe that he died in Mexico in 1845, but others think he made it back to Indian Territory and died in the Wichita Mountains.

CONCLUSION

I hope you enjoyed this journey through the lives of 32 of America's greatest heroes. Some of our heroes were people of actions, who fought and died for their beliefs, while others were academics and people of science who were far ahead of their time.

When you looked at the list, at first, you were probably taken by how different many of these people are from one another. You probably asked: what could Helen Keller and Al Capone possibly have in common and why are the Wright Brothers and Jesse James in the same book?

As you know now, the answer to those questions—just like American history—are a bit complicated. The simple answer is that all of the people in our book were true American originals who had great impacts on American history and, sometimes, on the world.

Beyond that, though, it's quite complex.

The truth is that the men and women in this book were heroes to a lot of people, but none of them were saints, with the possible exception of Helen Keller. All of the men and women in this book made their marks on the world during important times, not just in their lives, but in the history of the United States of America.

In the process of making their marks, all of these people developed a loyal following who began seeing them as heroes. As we discussed, even the outlaws and ones who fought against the government, such as Robert E. Lee, became heroes in the eyes of large segments of the American population.

And, most importantly, all of these people are still viewed as heroes by large segments of the American population.

The reality is that humans—no matter the place, time, or culture—need heroes.

They give us something to rally behind, believe in, and identify with. A hero like Thomas Edison or Alexander Graham Bell represents the inquisitive spirit in all of us, while Lewis and Clark, Neil Armstrong, and Charles Lindbergh capture the adventuresome human spirit and the will to push the limits. Helen Keller and George Washington are symbols of the honesty and goodness in all of us, while Al Capone, Jesse James, Robert E. Lee, and Sitting Bull appeal to that part of us that questions authority.

As American history continues to march on, no doubt many more people will be deserving of being on this list and there are, of course, plenty who could have been included already. Just remember, when you think about compiling your own list of great American heroes, there are as many different types of heroes as there are people.

DON'T FORGET YOUR FREE BOOKS

MORE BOOKS BY BILL O'NEILL

I hope you enjoyed this book and learned something new. Please feel free to check out some of my previous books on Amazon.

Made in the USA
Las Vegas, NV
22 November 2020